FROM AFRICA TO AMERICA

TWAYNE'S AFRICAN AMERICAN
HISTORY SERIES

Robert L. Harris, Jr., General Editor

FROM AFRICA TO AMERICA

African American History from the Colonial Era to the Early Republic, 1526–1790

WILLIAM D. PIERSEN

Twayne Publishers
An Imprint of Simon & Schuster Macmillan
New York

Prentice Hall International
London • Mexico City • New Delhi • Singapore • Sydney • Toronto

Twayne Publishers
An Imprint of Simon & Schuster Macmillan
1633 Broadway
New York, New York 10019

Library of Congress Cataloging-in-Publication Data

Piersen, William Dillon, 1942–
    From Africa to America : African American history from the Colonial era to the
early Republic, 1526–1790 / by William D. Piersen.
        p. cm. — (Twayne's African American History)
        Includes bibliographical references (p.) and index.
        ISBN 0-8057-3902-5 (alk. paper)
            1. Afro-Americans—History—To 1863.   I. Title.   II. Series.
E185.P49 1996   95-32327
973'.0496073—dc20   CIP

The paper used in this publication meets the minimum requirements of American
National Standard for Information Sciences—Permanence of Paper for Printed
Library Materials. ANSI Z3948–1984. ∞ ™

10 9 8 7 6 5 4 3 2   (hc)

Printed in the United States of America

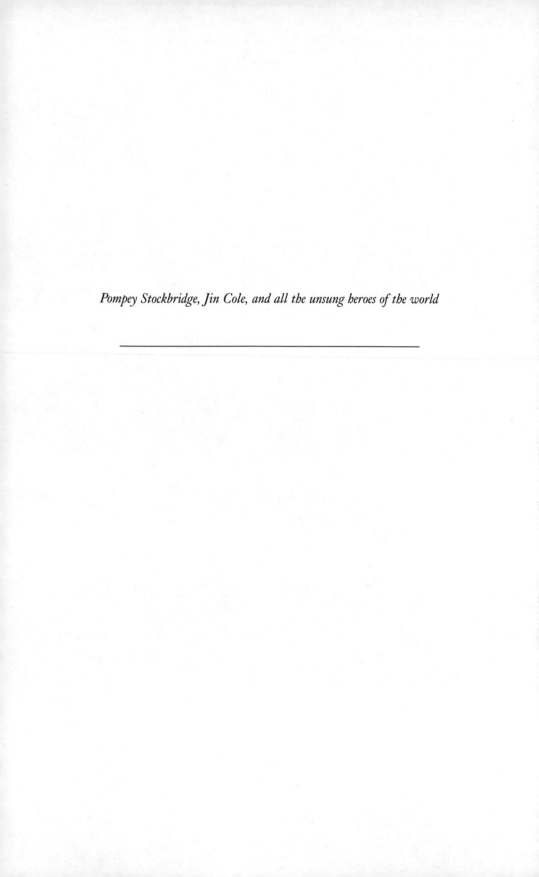

Pompey Stockbridge, Jin Cole, and all the unsung heroes of the world

Contents

Contents

VI

Looking Forward

TWENTY-ONE
New Directions in a New Nation

Preface

While hireling scribblers prostitute their pen,
Creating virtues for abandon'd men,
Ascribing merit to the vicious great,
And barely flatter whom they ought to hate—
Be mine the just, the grateful task to scan
Th' effulgent virtues of a *sable* man. . . .

Phillis Wheatley, "An Ode, On the Birthday of Pompey
Stockbridge" (c. 1770)

Phillis Wheatley had it right about historians. To read our nation's history, or any nation's history for that matter, is to spend far too much time with "the vicious great," whose violent and greedy deeds we "ought to hate." It would be far better to examine the lives of common men and women whose honest labors and noble aspirations more justly deserve our attention and emulation.

Twayne's new African American History Series, of which this book is a part, is intended, like Wheatley's poem, to right a wrong, to celebrate a sable heritage long washed out in the white glare of a thousand Founding Father monuments. Once the colonial era is examined from the shade of an African American perspective, the entire meaning of early American history takes a new focus, and the traditional Anglo-centered treatment of a national birth of political and economic freedom seems suspect and peculiarly interpreted.

In undertaking a reexamination of the colonial period, we are at a great disadvantage that Phillis Wheatley did not face. Wheatley knew her subject firsthand, yet we must rely on records prepared by the very people who despised Pompey Stockbridge and others of his kind; we must depend upon documents produced by people who found invisible the souls of their black laborers. To the white men who logged the colonial past in their court records, in their correspondence and diaries, and in their local histories and personal recollections, black slaves were barely worthy of notice except as problems. Thus, to understand colonial life in our own terms, we must look away from the perspectives tradition has given us. African American history has something new and unexpected to teach us about our nation's history, if only we ask the right questions.

The essential task of each generation of historians is far more to rethink the key issues than it is to replace the old evidence. Sometimes the result of this simple intellectual exercise is outraged surprise. So it might be, given our present understanding of freedom, if we were to ask, who were the real freedom fighters of the colonial era? African American history by its very nature brings an oppositional stance to the study of our nation's history, for, to paraphrase an old song, in America a white man's freedom has too often proved a black man's hell.

This book stands almost entirely on previously discovered evidence, on the hard labor and keen insights of dozens of my fellow historians. The volumes in this series, and certainly this book, are intended to pull together material on African American history published by a vast number of scholars in various journals and monographs; the intent is to make the results of such professional research more accessible to that great majority of people who do not spend their lives endlessly wandering down the dimly lit stacks of university libraries. As it is, I can cover but a small fraction of the new knowledge about African American colonial history that has been—and continues to be—developed.

I have tried to take an interpretive approach with this material, to look at the past from a perspective different from the one given to my generation. I have not centered on slavery as it was imposed on African Americans. Although what white people thought about their black fellow colonials, and what they did to them, was crucial to the African American experience, whites are not the focus of this volume. I am more interested here in blacks as builders of the new nation than in blacks as victims of it, although both themes are certainly illustrative of the same period.

Since Anglo-Americans and their politics are not my central theme, the geographical and chronological scope of this book is different from that of traditional colonial histories. Long before the English arrived in the lands that subsequently became the United States, Africans and Spaniards were already there. Therefore, the Spanish and French borderlands are included as part of the story of early African American settlement, just as they would be in any non-Anglocentric history of the colonial United States.

By looking at our nation's past in a new way, I hope to pass on to you a history of the colonial era that is more energizing than the traditional one, a history in which Africa joins our national bloodlines and at the end of which freedom is not yet defined as won. I will show you that some of the basic issues of the colonial era are still alive, that they even illuminate central questions of our own time. In that sense, history is never-ending. The past recedes behind us, ever widening like a wake roiling out across the waters, and each succeeding historian's question, like a shifting wind, writes new patterns on the seas of time.

Chronology of African American History
1526–1790

1526   Black slaves of Spain's Lucas Vásquez de Ayllón expedition to South Carolina and Georgia revolt; some settle among local Indians as the first nonnative settlers of what will become the United States.

1528   Estevanico, a Moroccan on the Pánfilo de Narváez expedition to Florida, escapes after capture by local Indians and with three Spaniards crosses the lower Gulf Coast region to Upper Mexico, reaching Mexico City in 1536.

1539   Estevanico is killed by Pueblo Indians while leading the explorations to New Mexico in search of the seven golden cities of Cibola.

1540   Blacks accompany the Spanish exploring expeditions of Alarcón, Coronado, and de Soto; a small number remain to settle in the lands that will become New Mexico, South Carolina, and Georgia.

1565   Saint Augustine founded by Spanish and African settlers.

1619   Twenty blacks from a Dutch slaver are purchased as indentured workers for the English settlement in Jamestown, Virginia.

1626   The first African slaves arrive in New Amsterdam (now New York City).

1641   Massachusetts explicitly permits slavery of Indians, whites, and Negroes in its *Body of Liberties.*

1642   When a French privateer brings to New Netherland some Negroes taken from a Spanish ship, they are sold as slaves because of their race, despite their claims to be free.

1652   Massachusetts enacts a law requiring all Negro and Indian servants to undergo military training so as to be able to help defend the colony.

1655   A free Virginia black, Anthony Johnson, successfully sues for the return of his slave John Casor, whom the court had earlier treated as an indentured servant.

1656   Fearing the potential for slave uprisings, Massachusetts reverses its 1652 statute and prohibits blacks from arming or training as militia. Connecticut, New Hampshire, and New York soon follow.

1662   Virginia reverses the presumption of English law that the child follows the status of his father and requires that children inherit the status of their mothers; mixed-race children of black mothers are thus enslaved.

1664   Maryland establishes slavery for life for Negroes and, to prevent white women from marrying black men, requires children to follow the status of their fathers.

1667   Virginia declares that baptism does not free a slave from bondage, thereby abandoning the Christian tradition of not enslaving other Christians.

1670   The Fundamental Constitutions of Carolina give every freeman "absolute power and authority over Negro slaves" in the colony.

1676   John Johnson, a third-generation free black, purchases a 44-acre tract in Maryland for a small plantation he calls Angola. Among the last rebel groups to surrender after Bacon's Rebellion in Virginia is an armed band of 80 blacks and 20 English. Virginia racial policies are subsequently designed to increase prejudice and keep the black and white poor from uniting.

1678   New Castle, Delaware, asks permission to trade with Maryland for slaves, "without which we cannot subsist."

1680   Domingo Navanjo, an Afro-Indian, helps lead the Pueblo Revolt, which drives the Spanish temporarily from New Mexico. To prevent insurrections, Virginia makes it illegal for blacks to arm themselves or leave their master's property without a pass.

1682   When William Penn and the Quakers first arrive in Pennsylvania, there are already blacks in the area working for Swedish, English, and Dutch settlers.

1693   The Negro Society of Boston is founded by black Christians to enhance the welfare of the city's slaves.

1700   The Bostonian Samuel Sewall publishes the first Anglo-American protest against slavery.

1706   An African slave teaches Cotton Mather an inoculation technique to fight smallpox. By 1776 George Washington will order that the entire Continental army be vaccinated by this method.

1708   Blacks become the majority population of South Carolina. New York passes its first act aimed at preventing the conspiracy of slaves and strengthens it two years later.

1712   Despite precautions, a slave revolt in New York results in the loss of 27 lives. Charleston, South Carolina, requires passes for blacks coming to town to celebrate on Sundays and holidays.

1720   A slave conspiracy is discovered in Charleston, South Carolina; the reputed leaders are burned, hanged, or banished. Some plan to escape through Creek territory to Saint Augustine.

1721   South Carolina establishes a treaty with the Creek Indians to pay for the return of Negro runaways, including the offer of one blanket in exchange for the head of any black killed during capture.

1723   To limit the free black population, Virginia makes it illegal to emancipate a slave without the consent of the governor and the governor's council.

c. 1730 A slave doctor in Louisiana uses citrus fruit in the first successful treatment of scurvy. After conducting questioning by torture, white leaders discover another potential slave uprising in Charleston, South Carolina, and execute the reputed leaders.

1731   Africans outnumber whites two to one in lower French-controlled Louisiana.

1738   The Pueblo de Gracia Real de Santa Terese de Mose, the first all-black city in territory that will become the United States, is built next to Saint Augustine.

1739   A major slave uprising led by a group of Angolans in Stono, South Carolina, results in more than 60 deaths.

1740   South Carolina adopts a slave code that greatly diminishes black freedom so as to reduce the probability of future rebellions.

1741   Fears of a slave conspiracy in New York result in 31 slave executions and 70 banishments.

1746   Blacks outnumber whites by more than two to one in French-controlled Natchez, Mobile, and the Illinois country.

1750   Georgia repeals its prohibition of slavery in the colony. After losing the *asientos de negros*—the exclusive right to take slaves to the Spanish colonies—British slavers begin offering more Africans at lower prices to their own colonies.

1751   South Carolina responds to the fear of poisoning by slaves by making it illegal for black doctors to administer any medicine except by white authority.

1755   Georgia adopts a slave code to reduce slave-owner cruelty and tighten controls on servants so as to reduce the chance of rebellion.

1760   Briton Hammon of Connecticut publishes the first African American slave narrative; Jupiter Hammon of New York publishes a poem in broadside.

1767   African-born Phillis Wheatley publishes her first poetry.

1770   The Afro-Indian Crispus Attucks is the first of five men killed in the Boston Massacre. Phillis Wheatley publishes a poem honoring the Rev. George Whitefield for his work with blacks.

1772   James Somerset, slave of a former Boston customs official living in England, successfully sues to prevent his master from taking him to Virginia. This was the beginning of the end of slavery in England.

1773   Massachusetts Negroes unsuccessfully petition the General Court for relief from bondage. Harvard students debate abolition at commencement. Blacks at Silver Bluff, South Carolina, establish the first Negro Baptist church at about this time. In Rhode Island, African-born John Quamine presents himself as a potential Congregational missionary to Africa but is turned down by church authorities.

1774   In his "Essay on Slavery," African-born Caesar Sarter argues that Massachusetts should free its bondspeople. Blacks unsuccessfully petition the General Court of Massachusetts to end slavery on the basis of all people's "natural right" to freedom. Thomas Gage, commander in chief of the British forces in America, receives two petitions from Massachusetts blacks requesting arms and offering troops to fight on the Loyalist side in exchange for freedom. In Georgia six newly arrived Africans incite a slave revolt in which four whites are killed; two of the black leaders are burned alive for retribution.

1775   Fifteen free blacks, after having their membership applications rejected by local white Masons, join a British army lodge in Boston and form African Masonic Lodge No. 1. Black soldiers fight as part of the American armies at Lexington and Concord. George Washington decides to permit no further enlistment of black troops into the Continental Army. Lord Dunmore, royal governor of Virginia, proclaims the freedom of all blacks who join the British forces.

1776   Fearing the effect Dunmore's proclamation will have on blacks alienated by Washington's exclusion of Negro soldiers, Congress again allows free blacks to enlist in the Continental Army. In Williamsburg, Virginia, a black Baptist called Moses organizes a church among the town's slaves. In Britain, Adam Smith's *Wealth of Nations* condemns slavery as an archaic, if profitable, mode of production.

1777   Vermont adopts a constitution that prohibits slavery.

1778   To entice blacks to enlist in Rhode Island's Black Regiment, slave recruits are unconditionally freed and given full army benefits. Following the decision in the Joseph Knight case in Scotland, slavery becomes illegal everywhere in the British home isles.

1779   Pompey Lamb guides Anthony Wayne's troops in their successful assault against Stony Point on the Hudson. New Hampshire Negroes unsuccessfully petition for emancipation on the basis of their natural right to freedom, but slavery for most New Hampshire blacks ends soon thereafter. Connecticut blacks unsuccessfully petition against what they argue is the great evil of slavery. Jean Baptiste Pointe Du Sable establishes a trading post that will become Chicago.

1780   Blacks in Newport, Rhode Island, form the Free African Union Society, a nationalist self-help organization. Pennsylvania passes the first state abolition law, but it emancipates no one immediately; instead, it frees slave children only after they have worked until they are grown. Massachusetts free blacks and mulattoes unsuccessfully petition for relief from taxation, claiming that there should be no taxation without representation and that they have been denied the privileges of citizenship.

1781   The Assembly of British East Florida promises freedom to slaves fighting with the British forces. Los Angeles, California, is founded by settlers of mixed African, Spanish, and Indian blood.

1782   Virginia reverses its statute of 1723 to permit private emancipation.

1783   Massachusetts courts interpret their state constitution of 1780 to have abolished slavery on the grounds that "all men are born free and equal"; those black males who pay taxes are given the right to vote. Maryland prohibits slave importation. Virginia frees all slaves who fought in the Continental Army.

1784   Methodists ban slaveholders from membership. Blacks around Saint Augustine enjoy religious freedom in their own Anabaptist church. Connecticut and Rhode Island pass acts for the gradual abolition of slavery. New Jersey frees all slaves who served in the Continental Army.

1785   Lemuel Haynes is ordained in Connecticut and takes the pulpit of a white church in Torrington. The New York Society for Promoting the Manumission of Slaves organizes; legislation for gradual emancipation passes the New York legislature.

1786   Legislation for gradual manumission passes in New Jersey. Several black groups in Boston petition the Massachusetts legislature for funds to return to Africa. Three hundred black troops who served with the British but never surrendered are defeated by Georgia and South Carolina militia guided by Catawba Indians.

1787   Richard Allen and Absalom Jones establish the Philadelphia Free African Society, precursor to the African Methodist Episcopal Church established in 1794. Congress prohibits slavery in the Northwest Territory, but fugitive slaves who reach there are to be returned to their owners. The Pennsylvania Abolition Society unsuccessfully petitions Congress to ban the slave trade. Delaware permits private emancipation of slaves. South Carolina prohibits importation of slaves. An African Free School is established in New York City with 40 students. Boston Negroes unsuccessfully petition for public schooling for the city's black children. The proposed national constitution overlooks the issue of bondage, never mentioning the word *slavery*, yet the overseas slave trade will continue for 20 years, fugitive slaves will be returned to claimants, and southern states will base representation in Congress on a count of all free people and "three fifths of all other persons."

1788   The First African Baptist Church of Savannah is organized under the leadership of Andrew Bryan. The Free African Union Society of Newport, Rhode Island, issues a call for the exodus of free blacks to Africa, but the Free African Society of Philadelphia is adamantly opposed. Boston's Black Masons successfully lead a fight to liberate three blacks who had been kidnapped and carried into West Indian slavery.

1789   Benjamin Banneker is selected to help survey the territory that will become the District of Columbia.

1790   Maryland permits private emancipation of slaves. In Charleston, South Carolina, free mulattoes organize the Brown Fellowship Society to provide education and welfare to the free black community. The African-born mathematical genius Thomas Fuller, known as the "African Calculator," dies in Philadelphia. Under pressure from the new U.S. government, Spain abandons its century-old policy of giving sanctuary to slaves who escape to Florida. Congress passes the Naturalization Law of 1790 specifying that only free white immigrants are eligible for naturalized citizenship. This racial restriction will remain in effect until 1952.

Introduction

If the black man is feeble and not important to the existing races, not on a parity with the best race, the black man must serve, and be exterminated. But if the black man carries in his bosom an indispensable element of a new and coming civilization; for the sake of that element, no wrong nor strength nor circumstance can hurt him; he will survive and play his part.

Ralph Waldo Emerson, "Emancipation in the British West Indies" (1844)

In point of fact, however, slavery and oppression may well have made black people more human and more American while it has made white people less human and less American. Anyway, Negroes have as much reason to think so as to think otherwise.

Albert Murray, *The Omni-Americans* (1970)

Only a little more than a generation ago most historians approached American colonial history as the story of a progressive awakening of democracy. Vast distances liberated colonial governments from imperial controls, unparalleled economic opportunities freed the energies and ambitions of common men, and a rapidly improving frontier lifestyle promoted social mobility and political optimism. The result was a revolutionary blossoming of democratic ideals, a new nation dedicated to the promise of human freedom.

Little attention was given to the experiences of darker peoples, whose lives did not seem to advance this grand drama of American freedom. The native peoples of America who were pushed aside or exterminated by the inrushing Europeans and the enslaved Africans whose labor produced so much of the colonial wealth upon which the new society was based were both relegated to the shadows, their stories made insignificant by what seemed the more important national saga of white settlers and their precedent-setting struggle for personal independence.

Today we carry a different vision of ourselves and our nation. Now a colonial history that overlooks the centrality of conquest and enslavement in the formation of the new American nation would seem terribly flawed. It is not that the basic values our nation celebrates have changed; the ideals of freedom are every bit as important to modern constructions of American history as ever. But no longer is the freedom story a hagiography dedicated to legendary Founding Fathers who grounded American nationalism on the bedrock of human liberty. Instead, for us, the leaders of the revolutionary generation seem all too human. Great but limited men, blindfolded by the class biases, racial narrowness, and sexism of their era, they were never able to even conceive the fuller and better implications of the American dream we now envision. It is true they gave us noble goals, but it is equally true they set us off down the wrong road toward reaching them.

The Native American and African heritages that proved so inconsequential to the historians of America's white supremacist past receive far more emphasis today, for as peoples of color have struggled successfully to assert themselves in the contemporary world, they inevitably have focused historical awareness on the darker peoples of the colonial era and their struggles for freedom as well. We now realize that an America built on slavery and near-genocide cannot also have been immaculately conceived out of the union of liberty and equality. Today we can see that a great price was paid for American freedom, and that it was not the white Founding Fathers who paid it. Fathers plan, and mothers give birth in sweat, blood, and pain. If we are heirs to the dreams of our white fathers, we are also the inheritors of the hopes and agony of our dark mothers. We will never be healthy as a nation until we acknowledge both sides of our lineage.

American historians have long neglected Africa's contribution to the new nation in part because of the profound ignorance of non-European peoples that marked an American historical education in our nation's more parochial days. African history just was not offered to American students. Since below the vast Sahara Desert the African continent lacked the written documents that Western scholars had been trained to evaluate as the stuff of history, what happened in precolonial Africa was judged to be neither historical nor important. As a result, Africa entered the American consciousness primarily as "the dark continent," a place victimized by the Atlantic slave trade, a supplier of labor—but not a mother culture for colonial America.

Why did earlier historians not look more closely? How could they misjudge the situation so badly? Western civilization's involvement with the Atlantic slave trade and Europe's imperialistic division of the African continent was far easier to justify if it was believed that Africans were capable of attaining only a primitive level of culture on their own. Thus, it should not be surprising that by the end of the nineteenth century a perverse reading of Western science had presented white scholars with what we now see was a racist, and wonderfully rationalizing, stereotype of Africa as a dark and backward continent. Early twentieth-century historians concluded—without thinking it necessary to examine the evidence—that nothing of cultural importance could have developed in black Africa; therefore, it followed that black Africans carried nothing of value to the New World besides their physical labor. American culture could have no significant African heritage.

Today historians are more cosmopolitan and look much further in their search for historical evidence, eagerly accepting the insights of such fields as archaeology, anthropology, folklore, and art history. As a result, there is now no doubt among serious historians that African societies have histories every bit as interesting and important as those of other regions across the globe. Without the pressure to continue to justify slavery and colonialism, Western scholars have been able to recalibrate the racist lens that so distorted our understanding of the African and American pasts.

As we have come to know a great deal about early African history and culture, our view of American history has changed. Both the original racist stereotyping of Africa and its reversal in our current appreciation of the African heritage have significant implications for our understanding of early American history. Traditionally the role of Africans in the colonial Americas was considered that of peripheral support labor. It was supposed that the brutalizing process of enslavement severed cultural memories of the old homelands; certainly those beliefs and customs that were not lost during the harsh Middle Passage must have disappeared in slavery—beaten out or erased by powerful forces of assimilation. The reality was far more complex.

Slavery did not turn Africans into helpless zombies wandering about in a daze of cultural amnesia. In actuality, whites and white ways were not all that impressive to black newcomers; neither were Africans so fragile or weak-willed that, faced with white hostility, they simply renounced the heritage of their old cultures. We now realize that Africans came from societies and civilizations of great complexity and significant accomplishment. Once we understand those original societies better, we can see that Africans carried with them many traditional ideas and customs that remained important to the lives of African Americans and to the colonies in which they settled.

Africans, too, were architects of the new American culture. Most were slaves, but that does not mean they were brute laborers working mindlessly under European orders. Colonial America was built as much by the intellect, the practical know-how, of Africans as by their physical exertions. The argument that African Americans were coequal builders of our national heritage is a major theme of this volume. There is no special pleading in this argument; colonial history can simply be neither understood nor appreciated without an awareness of the vital importance of African cultures and Africans in the formation of the new nation.

Race and culture have traditionally blurred together in American conversations about the black experience, and this fuzziness has set off an unending series of relatively unproductive debates in the field of Black Studies. When scholars consider a poem, for example, as "Black" poetry, is it Black because of its distinctive subject matter and voice or is it Black because of its author's race? In this book, the term *African American* is preferred because it permits a wider, less racialist focus than that usually connoted by the term *black*. The cultural-geographic meanings of *African American* are visible and obvious in the term itself; after all, culture, not color, is the driving force of history.

Therefore, although discussions of African American culture and history usually revolve around the lifestyles, arts, and historical experiences of people with racial ancestry from sub-Saharan Africa, it is far more precise to define African American culture as the historical development of a new way of life blending various African traditions with cultural elements from Europe and Native America. Moreover, the African American cultural legacy had a far broader impact on how colonial peoples lived in North America than racial definitions would imply, since aspects of African American culture were adopted by people across both racial and ethnic lines. In that sense, to become "American" in the colonial era was to become partly African American, no matter what one's racial heritage.

The Historiography of the Colonial Era

> Some time ago, I had the privilege of meeting at Cambridge, Mass., a group of about twenty-five young coloured men who were studying at Harvard University. . . . They knew a great deal about the local history of New England and were perfectly familiar with the story of Plymouth Rock and the settlement of Jamestown, and of all that concerned the white man's civilization both in America and out of America. But I found that through their entire course of training, neither in public schools, nor in the fitting schools, nor in Harvard, had any of them had an opportunity to study the history of their own race.
>
> Booker T. Washington, *The Story of the Negro* (1909)

The black Harvard students Booker T. Washington encountered in 1909 knew so little about African American history because it simply was not taught in American schools prior to the twentieth century. Although a few early black writers, such as William C. Nell (*The Services of Colored Americans in the Wars of 1776 and 1812*, 1851) and George Washington Williams (*History of the Negro Race in America*, 1882), saw the need for including the African American experience in our national history, their pioneering attempts at historical integration had little or no influence on the scholarly profession of history as a whole.

Not until 1911 would the first college course in African American history be offered, and when it was, the instructor was a sociologist, George Edmund Haynes of Fisk University, rather than a historian. In general, the intention of the small cohort of early African American historians was twofold: to suggest that the Negro (in the terminology of that generation) had a place in America's past by proving that black Americans were important to American history, and to demonstrate how quickly Americans of color assimilated into the mainstream. Such arguments were essential to assault demeaning racist myths about the Negro and his supposedly inconsequential historical role, which had been developed by white historians both to excuse the nation's caste system and to obscure rampant and long-standing abuses of the American ideals of liberty and individual worth.

A second generation of African American scholars followed up these early sorties with a full frontal offensive against the hitherto snow-blinded whiteness of the historical profession. Carter G. Woodson stood at the vanguard of this attack with his formation in 1915 of the Association for the Study of Negro Life and History (ASNLH) and the *Journal of Negro History*. In the following years every annual meeting of the ASNLH had sessions devoted to the teaching of African American history in both elementary and secondary schools. In an age of social and legal segregation, however, the lessons blacks were beginning to learn about their history in America and their contributions to the American way of life were generally ignored by the white scholars who still dominated the history profession.

It was not until around the Second World War that both white and black historians began rapidly to add color to the monochromatic story that previously had been generally perceived as American history. The implied questions about freedom and racial oppression that the Second World War was raising abroad had relevance to scholars trying to develop a more modern understanding of the American past at home, and these scholars quickly came to see American slavery as an important counterpoint to American freedom. Their new work clearly showed that the early history of our country had a brutal underside. While the colonial experience might have been liberating for most whites, it actively increased the oppression of almost all blacks.

In one sense, however, the postwar generation of historians of the African American experience still depended primarily on a single lens. Even as they examined the development of the legal and social bases of chattel slavery and exposed slavery's crucial importance to the American economy, they still approached their subject through the written records of the dominant class. Because whites remained the primary actors, the resulting histories were still artificially one-dimensional. Their interpretations may have been flipped, so that cruel white slaveholders replaced the freedom-loving Founding Fathers of earlier historians, but they still told a white-dominated story. Slavery was something done to blacks, and Africa was someplace out of which people were snatched. Such history had a white subject and a white verb; only the direct object was black.

Moreover, slavery in general histories was still interpreted primarily through the experiences of the 1850s. The first 200 years of American history were effectively ignored. Thus, when Louis R. Harlan wrote his *The Negro in*

American History in 1965 to guide teachers of American history, he included only one book devoted to the colonial era in his suggested bibliography. Such a late antebellum emphasis obscured just how pervasive slavery had been during the colonial era, how tightly it was connected to the revolutionary ideology of freedom, and how different bondage had been in the early years from what it would later become.

After the civil rights movement a new generation of scholars took up the task of rewriting the colonial history of African Americans. Led by Peter H. Wood's consideration of the black majority of colonial South Carolina, historians both white and black began arguing for the importance of the African heritage in understanding America. In this newer scholarship Africa was finally taken seriously as a place of national cultural origins.

In the work of modern historians, early African Americans are seen as more than a victimized people stripped of much of their cultural endowment; they are also understood to be culture bearers in their own right who shaped the development of the new nation far more than we had previously realized. The colonial era is no longer perceived culturally as simply a time of the dying out of African ways in a few lingering survivals. That was as much as people thought was possible when Melville Herskovits first suggested that African ideas and customs had crossed the Atlantic to America. But now much of the great cultural vigor of the colonial era is understood to have resulted from the multicultural interactions of the colonial frontier, including the powerful influences of a variety of societies from Africa.

The complexity of the many African heritages carried to the New World underlay the thousands of transformations that marked the development of a multiethnic African American way of life, the myriad of compromises that presaged the complex American story of our own times. As African cultures from the Senegambia blended in the New World with African cultures from the Gold and Slave Coasts, from the Bight of Benin and the ports of Kongo and Angola, something new and preeminently American was born. In English, Spanish, French, and Dutch colonial territories, and in contact with the native cultures of the East Coast, Gulf Coast, Mississippi River, and Southwest, African American culture was forming itself as something new, a veritable foreshadowing of the American experience.

Whereas European settlers first tried to maintain their old culture and ways of life but achieved only pallid and spindly imitations, African Americans from the first years created something recognizably new—a mixed culture of such enormous vitality that its arts and sensibilities would eventually come to dominate much of the artistic world of our own era.

Let us then see the colonial period for what it was: an era when peoples and ways of living collided, fracturing timeworn and comfortable patterns. The result was an unintended readjustment of older ways of thinking. As the Anglo-American elite discovered, successful colonization was impossible without African labor, but amassing wealth required that the fruits of this labor be expropriated to the benefit of the dominant class. Since old theories of nobles' rights and peasants' duties did not take root in America, a new rationale for economic and social inequality had to be developed.

Thus, an ideology defending a system of racial caste grew up within the same rapidly evolving milieu that was developing the political ideals of equality and democracy. The forced merger of the two antithetical principles into one national truth created a cultural schizophrenia, splitting American political ideology from American social reality in ways that still bedevil us. But at least people in our own times can see the glaring hypocrisy of Thomas Jefferson arguing with full conviction "that all men are created equal, that they are endowed by their Creator with certain unalienable Rights," and yet alienating those same rights every day by denying them to his black bondspeople.

From the African American perspective, the colonial struggles for better material conditions, increasing autonomy, political representation, and personal freedom were a reflection of the very marrow of their lives. In this, as in many other ways, African Americans were the quintessential pilgrims of the American dream. What whites said with their mouths, blacks knew from their souls; unfortunately, it took nearly 200 years for the political truth to surface. America could not be America until all Americans were free and equal.

Where our nation's whites too often simply avoided the contradictions between rhetoric and reality, blacks usually tried to reconcile them, and in the resulting dissonance they found the complex harmonies and haunting blue notes that have always energized the African American consciousness. It all began with the colonial era, over 200 formative years of African American history—as many years, incidentally, as are covered in all of the other seven volumes of this series combined.

Part One

Beginnings

one

The African Homelands

What is Africa to me:
Copper sun or scarlet sea,
Jungle star or jungle track,
Strong bronzed men, or regal black
Women from whose loins I sprang
When the birds of Eden sang?
One three centuries removed
From the scenes his fathers loved,
Spicy grove, cinnamon tree,
What is Africa to me?

Countee Cullen, "Heritage" (1925)

As a boy I had been accustomed to hear Africa referred to as one hears of Mexico, as if it were a place where a comparatively homogeneous people lives, having much the same customs, language, and civilization; in short, as if it were a country instead of a continent. It was some time before I was able to realize the vast extent and variety of the territory over which the dark races of Africa are spread. . . . I found also that I had only the vaguest notion of the multitude of different peoples that inhabit Africa and the variety of civilizations represented among its inhabitants.

Booker T. Washington, *The Story of the Negro* (1909)

Like Booker T. Washington, those who live outside Africa often think of the continent as a single place, and of Africans as a single people of a single race. But in fact Africa is a land of immense geographical and human diversity. In the era of the international slave trade Africa was the homeland of thousands of separate peoples, each with a distinct ethnicity and autonomous way of life.

3

For many years Western myths about the black continent portrayed Africa as a jungled land shrouded in mystery. But in truth only a small portion of historical Africa has ever been rainforest; far greater stretches of the vast land mass have always been sparsely vegetated grasslands lying parched for months under the relentless heat of a dry-season sun. Since Africa's geography has been so misleadingly stereotyped, it should not surprise us that there are similar misconceptions about Africa's peoples.

Indeed, a student trying to penetrate the truth of Africa might well feel a little like an eighteenth-century trader entering the river of a Joseph Conrad novel. The thick overgrowth and tangled vines of a century of racist thinking darken the sky as the scholar fights slowly upstream against a swirling current of ignorance. Swampy inlets on both sides form a maze of false channels, all leading relentlessly backward to stagnant pools festering with the racist legends of a "dark continent."

It is time to strike such phony, Hollywood-style backdrops. The mythic primitive rainforest that Europe envisioned as the heart of African darkness was always more a metaphoric representation of the tangled soul of white imperialism than an actual place somewhere in Africa. The real Africa was home to a multitude of distinctive, complex societies possessed of great social, political, and artistic sophistication. This Africa was the "old country" to many thousands of young men and women who were transported to new lives in colonial North America; the cultural heritages they carried with them from their motherlands contributed substantially to the development of the new American nation.

Although these new immigrants were forcefully separated by the slave trade from their homelands, their families, and their physical belongings, intellectually they did not forget who they were or where they came from. As Wolof, Fulbe, Bambara, Mandingo, Fante, and Fon, they arrived in America, carrying their cultural inheritance in both their minds and souls. As Yoruba, Igbo, Bakongo, Ovimbundu, and hundreds of other African nationalities, they landed on our shores enslaved but not destitute of memories.

What were these first African Americans like? To the English, who were just beginning to encounter the wider world, Africans appeared shockingly dark-skinned. Therefore, with exaggerated hyperbole, the British colonials called sub-Saharan Africans black people or Negroes (in much the same way Africans called the English "red men" or "whites"), but we must be aware that such generalized racial descriptions were a product of "they all look alike to me" insensitivity rather than true visual characterizations.

In reality, Africa's contribution to our nation's ancestral stock was made up of a diverse mixture of peoples. There was no single defining African color or shape. Among the arrivals from the western regions, for example, were brownish-red, wavy-haired Fulani whose physical characteristics were every bit as indigenously African as those of the ebon-purple residents of the Congo Basin in Central Africa. Africans imported to America were tall and slender

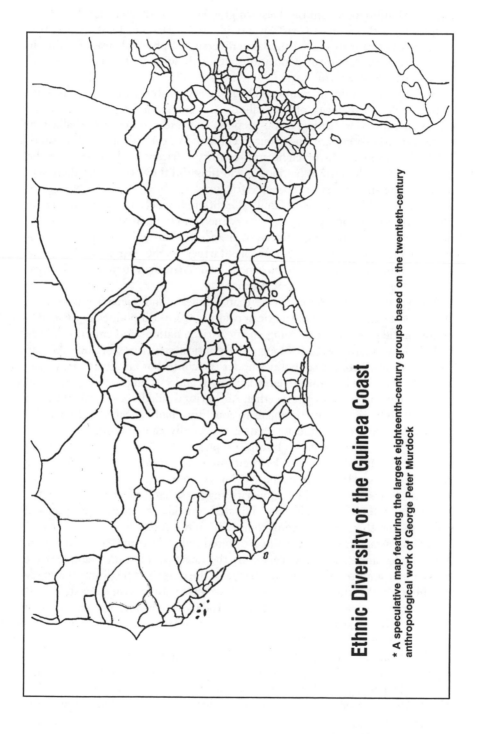

Ethnic Diversity of the Guinea Coast

* A speculative map featuring the largest eighteenth-century groups based on the twentieth-century anthropological work of George Peter Murdock

like the Mandingoes from the Western grasslands, or shorter and darker like peoples from the Guinea Coast, or anywhere in between. In short, the first African Americans displayed the same diversity of physical types we find in today's African American population, although without the European and Native American intermixture.

Socially the continent exhibited a complexity as abundant as the diversity of its peoples. A majority of colonial-era Africans were farmers, but enough others specialized in fishing, cattle-keeping, and trade and craft specialization to disarm any generalizations about livelihood. We can ask simple questions: What did seventeenth- or eighteenth-century Africans look like? How did they make their livings? What kind of clothing did they wear? But there will never be one single answer to fit all Africans.

Even something as basic as family life differed widely from people to people. Thus, during the eighteenth century men and women of the Akan-speaking groups of the Gold Coast traced their ancestry through their mothers' relatives, while among the Hausa peoples farther to the east inheritance was traced through the fathers' kin. No single, basic African system of family organization was carried to America, but many.

Politics were even more diverse than ethnicity and social arrangements. When the 13 British North American colonies were still politically divided, a nation in the process of becoming, many African nations and empires already had histories many centuries long. The political structures of such African societies ranged from small polities under the control of family elders, village councils, and local headmen to large kingdoms and vast empires larger than all the 13 American colonies put together. Authority resided in everyone from kin leaders who were first among equals to constitutionally checked and balanced royal executives, to absolute autocrats and even divine emperors.

Despite the continent's political complexity, Europeans found Africa's political institutions enough like their own that they rarely characterized African politics as bizarre or exotic, as they so often did Africa's social customs and indigenous religions. This similarity suggests that Africans arriving in the American colonies would have adjusted quickly to European political notions—and that, indeed, seems to have been the case.

African arts, like African politics, differed radically from region to region. The wooden ancestral figures carved by the forest peoples, for example, were of no importance to peoples on the fringe of the deserts. The drums that were ubiquitous in the music of the Guinea Coast gave way to stringed instruments farther into the grasslands of the Sudan. Today we consider it axiomatic that our artistic heritage as a nation has deep roots in Africa, but from which parts of Africa did it spring?

Despite all these complexities, our task of coming to a general understanding of the African contribution to colonial American history is not as daunting as it might first appear, for most of the African peoples who were carried to North America as slave labor came primarily from the coastal and connecting interior regions of West and West Central Africa. And in these regions there was enough cultural similarity that many generalizations are possible.

Precisely because the Africans who came to England's North American colonies brought much from their old ways of life with them, then blended those old ways with what they encountered in the colonies to help build the new nation, it is worth looking more closely at the traditional West African cultures in the ancestral homelands of today's African Americans.

two

Life in the West African Grasslands

> The Negroes [of Mali] possess some admirable qualities. They
> are seldom unjust, and have a greater abhorrence of inequity
> than any other people. Their sultan shows no mercy to any one
> guilty of the least act of injustice. There is complete security in
> their country. Neither traveller nor inhabitant has anything to
> fear from robbers or men of violence. They do not confiscate the
> property of any white man who dies in their country, even if it
> be uncounted wealth. On the contrary, they give it into the
> charge of some trustworthy person among the whites, until the
> rightful heir takes possession. They are careful to observe the
> hours of prayer, and assiduous in attending them in congrega-
> tions, and in bringing up their children.
>
> The traveler Ibn Baṭṭūṭah, on the people of Mali (1352)

Some 5,000 years ago, in the great West African savanna below the Sahara
Desert, local peoples began to experiment with the farming techniques that
would make the region one of the world's rare cradles of agriculture. Along
and near the watered banks of the great River Niger, farmers learned to cultivate indigenous crops of millet, sorghum, and African rice. This transition
from hunting and gathering to stable farming, in turn, allowed early small-
scale states to form across the grasslands even before the rise of the Roman
Empire.

When trans-Saharan trade increased 2,000 years ago with the expansion of
camel-herding peoples into the Sahara Desert, much larger states began to form.
These new governments arose out of the need to provide protected markets to
facilitate the sale of goods that had been carried hundreds of miles from the geographically distinct lands to the north and south. In the centrally located

grassland trading cities, gold and kola brought up from the forests were exchanged for salt carried down on camels from the Sahara or for luxurious foreign goods carried at great expense across the vast desert from rich civilizations to the north and east.

The trading cities of the West African savanna pumped the economic lifeblood of the great golden empires remembered as ancient Ghana, Mali, Songhay, and Kanem-Bornu. These legendary imperial states reached the zenith of their power from the thirteenth to the sixteenth centuries by exploiting the local agricultural surplus and dominating the international trade of West Africa. To control the two economic spheres of farming and commerce, the grasslands empires modified the traditional West African political organization of the agriculturalists by importing urban bureaucratic and commercial structures from North Africa to improve record-keeping and codify the laws of commerce around the universal system of Islam.

From the countryside such urban changes were invisible for the most part, and political administration over the farmers remained grounded in traditional religious beliefs that honored the sovereignty of founding ancestors and the guiding spirits of the land. But in the cities a cosmopolitanism was developing as the religion of Islam shaped a new way of life that was not only attractive to traders from North Africa but capable of unifying the diverse pagan peoples of the grasslands into a single political realm.

To the farming peoples the imperial monarchs of the great grasslands empires were divine kings responsible for the spiritual health of their domains and their subjects; for the merchants and city dwellers, however, their rulers were defenders of the Muslim faith, principally responsible for providing the stability and righteous social order necessary for international commerce.

Slaves had a place in the great grasslands empires, but not at all the same place they would have in the English North American colonies. In West Africa slaves were treated as people, not property. Muslim-owned slaves were as likely to serve as bureaucrats or professional soldiers as agricultural laborers. They made excellent officials and were commonly appointed to be military commanders because as slaves they owed allegiance to the ruler alone; they had no conflicting loyalties to subservient nobles or particular regions or peoples. Moreover, as outsiders lacking freedom, slave officeholders and soldiers could not threaten to seize power and thus weaken imperial rule.

In general, the number of people in bondage increased as the size of the states expanded, for ownership of slave workers reduced a ruler's dependence on the labor reserves of nobles, who provided help only in response to specific requests. Many of the slave workers were sent to live under the command of royal wives in special agricultural villages designed to free rulers from overdependence on the feudal food tributes taken from local peoples.

The result of such imperial developments was a series of expansive West African empires whose wealth and hospitality won well-deserved international renown. Just how impressive these empires were can be seen in the story of

Mansa Mūsā, a ruler of Mali who went on a pilgrimage to Mecca in 1324. Lord Mūsā was said to have crossed the vast Sahara Desert with an entourage of 60,000 people; securing supplies and water for such an impressive international venture is as mind-boggling today as it would have seemed then. But when Mūsā's party arrived in Egypt, their entrance was triumphal rather than ragged: 500 men preceded the king in a grand procession, each carrying a staff of pure gold. The great Mūsā had arrived.

Mansa Mūsā's emphatic attention to showy displays of wealth during his Egyptian sojourn suggests that his trip was clearly more than a religious pilgrimage by a humble pilgrim; in fact, the expedition appears to have been an advertising venture of gigantic and international proportions. To cover his expenses and call attention to the abundant prosperity of his homeland, Mūsā brought along 27,000 pounds of gold dust, and his party's lavish tipping and extravagant shopping in the international city of Cairo inflated prices there, destabilizing the tourist economy for years to come.

Not surprisingly, news of these activities soon spread, and the image of the great Mūsā with an immense nugget of gold in his hand soon appeared on a European map with the inscription: "This negro lord is called Mūsā Mali, Lord of the Negroes of Guinea. So abundant is the gold which is found in his country that he is the richest and most noble king in all the land."[1]

No wonder that European interest in West Africa perked up. The desire for West African gold ignited a powerful lust in the poorer regions to the north. It was the hunger for new commerce and cheap gold that first drove European merchants to the African coast, not an interest in slave labor, but the tides of history were about to change. With the Spanish retaking of Granada from the North African Moors in 1492, the age of African imperialism in southwestern Europe ended, and almost immediately the voyages of Christopher Columbus opened a new world of opportunities in the Americas for the maritime states of western Europe, which were even then in the process of developing trade contacts along the coast of West Africa.

The African story in America, however, may predate the voyages of Columbus and the end of African imperialism in the Spanish lands, for there is suggestive evidence, as Ivan Van Sertima and others have shown, that small numbers of Africans may have arrived in the Americas more than 2,000 years before Columbus. Gigantic stone heads and terra-cotta sculpture with Negroid-looking features from the early Olmec civilization along the east coast of modern-day Mexico suggest a small but significant African presence in the Central American region from as early as the end of the Egyptian era. Controversial skeletal remains from pre-Columbian burials in Pecos Pueblo along the Texas–New Mexico border likewise suggest a Negroid intrusion into that region, perhaps from the nearby Olmec area.

While the case for such early African-Olmec contact is still speculative, other evidence, even stronger, suggests that later Africans also may have made pre-Columbian voyages to the Americas. In 1325 Lord Mūsā of Mali, while in

Cairo on his famous pilgrimage, gave an interview to a local scholar explaining that he had come to rule Mali only after the preceding monarch had been lost on a large, well-supplied expedition to cross a great sea—which must have been the Atlantic Ocean. This sketchy tale of pre-Columbian explorations dwarfing the efforts of the famous Italian navigator ironically finds later corroboration in the testimony of Christopher Columbus himself.

Columbus reported having been told by the local peoples of Hispaniola in the Caribbean that black people had arrived there before him from the southeast. They were said to have carried spears tipped with precious metals like those we now know were used in the Malian court. Moreover, during a later voyage to the Cape Verde Islands in the Atlantic, southwest of Europe, Columbus was told by islanders that canoes from the coast of Guinea had arrived filled with merchandise for trade long before the famous Italian explorer made his first Atlantic crossing.

The logic that drove Columbus to sail directly west toward Asia so as to bypass the thousands of middlemen who made the eastern trade so expensive would have been as apparent to an Africa ruler of the great trading empire of Mali. Unfortunately for the Malians, however, their large fleet of exploring ships would have been developed, like most boats of West African nautical design, for river travel. The result seems to have been that travel in the direction of wind and current toward the Americas was far easier for African explorers than the return voyage home. Their difficulty in returning was probably the reason Africa's earliest contacts with the Americas never assumed the importance of later European ventures.

Too often we consider the arrival of Africans in the Americas only as slaves. It would be more historically accurate to recall that Africans probably first entered the Americas as explorers sailing under African flags. They next arrived as members of Spanish expeditions of conquest and exploration, and it was only after centuries of black pioneering that other Africans would come to English North America in the role of enslaved agricultural laborers.

One of the key reasons black labor became so widely used in the North American colonies was that Africans were highly skilled in the tasks of colonization. Of the peoples influenced by the grasslands cultures, it was those at the western edge in the Senegambia region, far more than those from the interior, who were taken in bondage to North America. Senegambians were highly valued in North America because they already possessed the economic skills required for successful development of the southeastern colonies.

Most of the plants that would later become the major export crops of the English North American colonies were farmed in Senegambia. The rice and indigo that would become so important in both South Carolina and Louisiana were Senegambian specialties; in addition, by the time slave imports to English North America became important, maize, peanuts, and tobacco—crops originally brought from the Americas—were harvested on the Windward Coast along with native melons, gourds, beans, cotton, sorghum, and millet.

Farmwork in the lands of West Africa was hard because of the heat and because plows could not be used in the sub-Saharan lands: the thin soil cover would have been damaged by deep tillage. Workers hoed in a fatiguing stooped position using a short-handled tool so that they could strike the soil with great force and precision. To make the work more endurable, people often worked together in the fields to the rhythms of improvised songs.

Day-to-day field chores were typically the responsibility of women, whose busy days also included the traditional female domestic obligations of washing, child-rearing, food preparation, and cooking. Men usually had more leisure time. In the periods when men worked the hardest, such as when they cleared land for new fields or performed civic functions, they usually organized their efforts in work groups with other men from their village compounds or age-grade associations.

The women of the West African savannas commonly draped themselves in flowing robes made up of two large pieces of cotton cloth, often dyed a beautiful indigo blue; one they wrapped around their waists and draped to their ankles, the other they wore thrown over their shoulders. In the tropical heat it was important to loosely cover the body, and women also wound narrow cotton bands around their heads, forming attractive headcloths, to protect themselves from the blazing sun. Men of the region typically wore white cotton caps, loose frocks and trousers of the same material reaching to their knees, and sandals to protect their feet.

The majority of the people in the regions of Africa that supplied slaves to North America were agriculturists. Many of the local peoples were also skilled, however, in tending livestock, especially cattle, sheep, and goats; others were master blacksmiths who made practical tools, such as knives, hatchets, and axes, as well as fine jewelry, such as the gold pins with which the women decorated their hair. Pottery-making, woodworking, leather-working, and cotton-weaving were all usually under the control of craft specialists; as a result, the productions of the African coast were of very high quality. Skilled boatbuilders, canoemen, traders, and fishermen worked the rivers as well as the deeper ocean. Most men were also wise in the stratagems of trapping and hunting small and medium-sized game; special hunting societies were often formed for capturing larger animals.

The women of Senegambia spun the region's cotton fibers into threads that were then woven into cloth and dyed with indigo to create the beautiful blue robes for which the region was famous. Many women traded in the local markets, and during the years of the Atlantic trade an elite among these trading women married visiting European merchants, thereby founding great mercantile families that dominated the Windward Coast's side of the oceanic commerce.

Society in Senegambia was divided into three main classes. The majority of people at the top were free citizens and mostly small farmers; of slightly lower repute, and far fewer in number, were members of the endogamous families, which followed special caste occupations such as blacksmith, leatherworker, woodworker, and minstrel. On the bottom rung of society resided a lower class of servile laborers whom we might call slaves. But in Senegambia, where neither wealth nor status aligned itself precisely by class, there was much overlapping of the three main classes. Moreover, a person's primary status came by way of kinship—not economic or occupational position.

Most of the region's slaves had traditionally entered society as complete outsiders, most often as foreigners captured in war. Such slaves, like those purchased in trade, had few or any rights in societies where lineage usually defined social status. Those servants born into their masters' families, however, were in a very different situation, for they were becoming quasi-kinsmen, and slave wives who produced children for their husband-masters were often freed. According to Francis Moore, who lived for a period in early eighteenth-century Senegambia:

> Several of the Natives have many Slaves born in their Families. . . . And tho' in some Parts of Africa they sell their Slaves born in the Family, yet in the River Gambia they think it a very wicked thing; and I never heard of but one that ever sold a Family-Slave, except for such Crimes as would have made them to be sold had they been free. If there are many Family-Slaves, and one of them commits a Crime, the Master cannot sell him without the joint Consent of the rest; for if he does, they will all run away, and be protected by the next kingdom, to which they fly.[2]

In a time before the wage economy, when people's time could not be bought and sold, purchasing slaves was the quickest and easiest way to fill expanding labor needs. Additionally, many of the region's soldiers were slaves; the officers among such slave troops had enormous power and authority despite their servile origins. Sometimes bondspeople worked in separate villages, where they lived like feudal peasants: their lives were in many ways like those of free people except that they owed part of their harvest to their lords. Other slaves worked directly under their masters, meeting whatever labor needs existed. It is important to note that the West African system of unfree labor was quite different from that which developed in North America, but it is just as important to understand that its existence opened the way for the Atlantic slave trade and the forms of labor exploitation that would develop in the English colonies.

In Senegambia, inheritance had traditionally passed through the woman's line, but as the social currents of Islam spread westward with Mande-speaking traders and farmers after the fourteenth century, some peoples began to take up patrilineal descent. Whether matrilineal or patrilineal, people identified themselves as members of large clans that provided them with their surnames and traced group ancestry back to the legendary past. Everyone within the clan was treated as kin and shared a respect for the clan's totemic animal, which they would never harm, for it was a symbol of the clan's corporate nature and a bond to the other living things of the earth.

In day-to-day life most social activities were based on smaller segments of the larger clans, such as members of an extended family living together in one location. These lineage subsegments of the larger clan commonly symbolized their kinship spatially by forming housing compounds wherein the small abodes of a husband and his wives—if he was rich enough to have more than one wife—were placed next to those of related lineage kinsfolk (each adult having his or her own small sleeping quarters) so as to create a family ward within a larger town or village.

The homes themselves were usually very small and dark, with an open door to let in the light and an unwelcome plague of mosquitoes during the wet season. Most households had few furnishings: a bed laid upon branches supported by forked posts set into the floor, a clay water jar, some pots and calabashes, and perhaps a wooden chest and stool. To keep the air fresh people often kept a kind of potpourri of bagged sweet gums, which could also be tossed on the fire at night. Because of the heat, people spent their days and early evenings outdoors as much as possible. In the dry season the old men sitting and talking in the shade of a great tree in the village center would watch the women glide by carrying heavy loads balanced upon their heads, while nearly naked children, laughing, giggling, and gray with dust, scrambled back and forth engaged in their games.

To a great extent, status in society came from seniority and age. The old men may well have been talking politics, since the oldest members of the ward usually represented their kinspeople in discussions with local officials; the elders were also expected to settle family disputes and oversee the collection and redistribution of the lineage's collective economic efforts. Castes of craft specialists such as blacksmiths and wood-carvers, and poorer people who attached themselves to great men as clients and slaves also lived in the village wards. The status of the members of these social groups depended to a great extent on the honor attaching to their particular lineage hosts or masters.

Although by the beginning of the Atlantic slave trade, around 1450, Muslim merchants from the interior empires had long been visiting the societies along the western coast, sometimes settling with their families, most of the local peoples still practiced polytheistic local religions whose highest gods were believed to be remote from their human children. Nonetheless, both gods and nature spirits were believed to enter into devotees during intense religious dancing or during certain divination rites. In daily life, however, most people paid greatest attention to a wide and continually changing set of rituals designed to honor or appease ancestral and nature spirits that might otherwise harm supplicants and their families. Almost everyone carried small charms that were believed to protect their owners from evil and misfortune.

Religion was a vital part of everyday life and therefore not isolated in a separate holy building or confined to a special day of the week. There was no priestly class as there was in Christian Europe or English North America, although African doctors had to be religious specialists as well as experts in psychology and pharmacology because diagnosis and healing were believed to require supernatural as well as medicinal intervention. It was generally believed on the western coast that young healthy people did not get sick unless a supernatural force had been disturbed and was working against them. Thus, the power of magic became intertwined with the power of religion.

West Africans did not believe in a personal savior or a devil; instead, they accepted that they lived in an often disorderly universe made more uncertain by capricious spirits, witchcraft, and magic. Yet they were also confident that the life given to humans was good and that whatever twists and turns life took, an ultimate, irresistible fate determined human destiny.

Holidays were marked by dancing, with the best dancers often wearing small bells tied to their arms and legs so the rhythms would harmonize with the accompanying drums. Local beers were served, and the men especially enjoyed the wrestling matches between village champions that were featured during grand occasions.

Many aspects of the cultural life of the interior grasslands and Senegambia would be carried to America and become commonplaces of early African American life. But in English North America the customs of the grasslands had to blend not only with new European customs but with other African ways of life imported from the forest regions of the more southerly western coast.

three

Life in the Forest Regions of West and Central Africa

> I was born at Dukandarra, in Guinea, about the year 1729. My
> father's name was Saungm Furro, Prince of the tribe of
> Dukandarra. My father had three wives. Polygamy was not
> uncommon in that country, especially among the rich. . . . By his
> first wife he had three children. The eldest of them was myself,
> named by my father, Broteer. . . . I descended from a very large,
> tall and stout race of beings, much larger than the generality of
> people in other parts of the globe, being commonly considerable
> above six feet in height, and every way well proportioned.
>
> The New England slave Venture Smith, *A Narrative of the Life
> and Adventures of Venture* (1798)

Most of the ancestors of contemporary African Americans did not come from
the grasslands empires of West Africa and their hinterlands in Senegambia but
from the forest regions along the great bend of the western coast where the
dense tropical forests hindered communications and made large imperial-sized
states virtually impossible. In the wetter forest regions people customarily lived
as small-scale subsistence farmers with their political lives organized around
kinspeople and fellow villagers. The small villages and tiny states of the forests
were at the farthest and poorest ends of the long-distance trade routes that fed
the imperial international trade of the African grasslands.

In the forest societies local trading was for the most part in the hands of
women, who also oversaw agricultural production. Although males worked
cooperatively at the start of the growing season to clear fields around the villages and burn brush, they soon settled back into a life of relative ease while

women took over the day-to-day tasks of tending the crops. Since tropical soils were so quickly exhausted, new brush-covered lands had to be cleared yearly; after several years' use, the old plots needed time to lie fallow and recover.

Because of the constant shifting of fields within large reserves of fallow brushland, individual land ownership of private plots was not economical in the forested regions of West Africa; instead, land was held communally and redistributed by kin groups to individuals on the basis of need. People settled in central villages comprising closely clustered housing compounds rather than on isolated individual farmsteads, which would soon have been in fields no longer cultivated. As a result, forest life was characterized by intense social interactions, especially between kinspeople who shared a common ancestry, whether through paternal or maternal lineage. Because people had to live so closely together, manners and socially approved behaviors were rigorously enforced by intense pressure from both families and the wider community.

In the same way, since the economic life of the forest regions revolved around the cultivation of family landholdings, most important economic decisions were made within the councils of the large extended families. The older members of kin groups were considered the wisest and most deserving of respect; their opinions carried the most weight. People did what was required of them because it was their family responsibility. This attitude prevailed even in religion: deceased ancestors were believed to be actively watching over the living, helping their heirs when asked, and punishing them with misfortune and illness if they strayed from the course of proper social and family conduct.

When the needs of the community crossed family lines, new forms of social organization took over. Secret societies that represented the power of the ancestors or other spiritual forces brought together men and women of various lineages and clans. In areas where political authority was weak, the social authority of the secret societies to hold communities together and reinforce proper modes of behavior was especially strong. Unlike life outside the societies, group members could rise to the top ranks on the basis of their individual abilities rather than primarily by seniority or family status. The groups' public presentations, which featured both fearsome and humorous maskers, were an important part of all holiday celebrations.

Traditional forms of slavery in the region developed out of the need to incorporate outsiders, such as prisoners of war, into the predominantly kin-based social systems. As Ibo-born Olaudah Equiano explained:

> Those prisoners which were not sold or redeemed we kept as slaves: but how different was their condition from that of the slaves in the West Indies! With us they do no more work than other members of the community, even their master; their food, clothing and lodging were nearly the same as theirs (except that they were not permitted to eat with those who were freeborn), and there was scarce any other difference between them than a superior degree of importance which the head of a family

possesses in our state, and that authority which, as such, he exercises over every part of his household. Some of these slaves have even slaves under them as their own property and for their own use.[1]

Prior to the Atlantic commerce, slavery was neither particularly important nor overly harsh in the forest regions. The institution would later be exploited, however, by Africans and foreigners alike, and in its more virulent form African slavery became a curse to both the continent and the people like Olaudah Equiano who were sent off into the Atlantic diaspora.

Although by the seventeenth century royal political organizations were becoming more common in the expanding states of the forest regions, the basic democratic principles of local life endured. Kings were usually elected from candidates among a large royal family (unlike their European counterparts, who were elevated on the basis of seniority and consanguinity no matter what their competence). On the village level, most day-to-day political decision-making required family consensus.

Because the hot, humid climate made the long-term preservation of agricultural and other surplus extremely difficult, status in the forest societies was acquired more by redistributing wealth than by accumulating it. Since a large family was the mark of a great man or woman, people strove to expand their families as fast or faster than their wealth. This practice promoted relatively egalitarian living conditions, since a richer man had to divide his assets among more dependents. It also kept the emphasis on social obligations rather than on self-interest.

Much like the rural peoples of colonial North America, most African families tried to be as economically self-sufficient as possible. With the help of kinspeople, adults built their own houses, most with thatched roofs made from palm leaves. No single style of housing was common to all the forest societies. In Dahomey mud-walled houses predominated; nearby the Yoruba built their walls with large earthen bricks; to the southeast the Ibo used wattle-and-daub construction; even farther south the Bakongo interlaced prefabricated palm branches and leaves to quickly form walls and roofs.

The diets of most forest farmers revolved around palm oil and highly caloric (but not very nutritional) yams. Stews were commonly prepared from both ingredients, along with peas, beans, melon seeds, onions, and okra, and then highly seasoned with peppers. After a long, slow cooking, the stew was poured into a large calabash platter and served with a loaf of a warm doughy yam paste called *fufu*. After washing their hands, diners would squat around the common calabash to eat. Many people would begin the meal by pouring out a small quantity of the food as a libation to the spirits of the ancestors, after which they would take turns breaking off pieces of fufu to form into small balls for soaking up the tasty stew. In most societies women and children, as well as slaves, were expected to eat separately from the men.

Olaudah Equiano has left us a good description of day-to-day life among his Ibo people of the early eighteenth century:

> As our manners are simple, our luxuries are few. The dress of both sexes are nearly the same. It generally consists of a long piece of [cotton cloth] wrapped loosely round the body . . . this is usually died blue, which is our favourite colour. It is extracted from a berry [indigo], and is brighter and richer than any I have seen in Europe. Besides this, our women of distinction wear golden ornaments . . . on their arms and legs. When our women are not employed with the men in tillage, their usual occupation is spinning and weaving cotton, which they afterwards dye, and make into garments. They also manufacture earthen vessels [and tobacco pipes] of many kinds.[2]

Traditionally the troops of the forest states armed themselves with spears, bows and arrows, daggers, and swords. The regional craftsmanship in wood and metal work was very high quality, and most weapons were of local manufacture until European-made guns began to be imported in considerable numbers in the seventeenth and eighteenth centuries. By the time large numbers of slaves were imported into English North America, the coastal societies were extremely well armed and most local infantrymen carried muskets.

Although the forest states were not particularly impressive by international standards of size, wealth, or military strength, they fostered one of the world's great traditions in the visual and musical arts. The religiously oriented wooden sculpture and masks they designed to emphasize fertility and the power of the ancestors helped shape the abstract vision that characterizes most of today's modern art, while the complex and improvisational musical and dance styles that originated in the forest regions were the progenitors of the African-American musical and dance forms that have come to dominate much of the modern world.

In his recollections of his African childhood, Olaudah Equiano emphasized the importance of the arts to his Ibo people and the region as a whole:

> We are almost a nation of dancers, musicians, and poets. Thus every great event, such as a triumphant return from battle, or other cause of public rejoicing, is celebrated in public dances, which are accompanied with songs and music suited to the occasion. The assembly is separated into four divisions which dance either apart or in succession, and each with a character to itself. . . . Each [dance] represents some interesting scene of real life, such as a great achievement, domestic employment, a pathetic story, or some rural sport; and, as the subject is generally founded on some real event, it is therefore ever new. This gives our dances a spirit and variety which I have scarcely seen elsewhere. We have many

musical instruments, particularly drums of different kinds, a piece of music which resembles a guitar, and another much like a [xylophone].[3]

The artistic heritage that Equiano described easily merged with similar ones from other West African nations and would be familiar to any student of early African American culture, although the drums he mentioned would have to be downplayed in North America.

Although the people of West Africa did not carry their material wealth to the Americas, they brought with them assets far greater in terms of cultural wealth, an inheritance upon which much of the best of American artistic achievements still depend. In this sense, certainly, African Americans were not stripped of their cultural heritage. But the individual heritages that West Africans carried with them across the ocean had to change when they inter-mixed with other African peoples in the Americas and interacted with Native and European Americans as well. The result was a new cultural and artistic style that, because of the mixing, was far more accessible to non-Africans and thus ultimately far more influential in the world at large.

four

The East Atlantic Slaving System

I, young in life, by seeming cruel fate
Was snatch'd from *Afric's* fancy'd happy seat:
What pangs excruciating must molest,
What sorrows labour in my parent's breast?
Steel'd was that soul and by no misery mov'd
That from a father seiz'd his babe belov'd.
Such, such my case. And can I then but pray
Others may never feel tyrannic sway?

Phillis Wheatley, "To the Right Honourable William, Earl of
Dartmouth, His Majesty's Principal Secretary of State for
North America" (1773)

Africa entered the sixteenth century enjoying an age of relative peace and prosperity. The recent expulsion from European Iberia of the Moors of the North African Almohad empire did not seem particularly threatening, for no foreign power had ever successfully invaded the interior of Africa. The majority of Africans were subsistence farmers, living in small, relatively egalitarian societies, unaware that a great storm from the northwest was about to disrupt their world and change their lives forever.

That the distant thunder from the north was still unnoticed is not so surprising, for western Europe was just emerging from a long history of underdevelopment. Moreover, the small and undistinguished Portuguese nation, which would first turn Europe's disadvantages into opportunities, was isolated on the Atlantic coast, far from the rich Mediterranean commerce. Yet the Portuguese put what they learned from their difficult location on the Atlantic together with nautical insights gained on the Moorish frontier to develop the caravel, a new form of warship sturdy enough to withstand ocean storms and therefore strong enough to carry heavy guns and survive the terrible shocks of their recoil.

Originally the Portuguese had only a minor interest in West Africa; their primary intention was to turn the Moorish flank by sailing around the continent to the riches of Asia. When Vasco da Gama rounded the horn of South Africa in 1498 and with incredible good fortune reached India, he lost two-thirds of his men and half of his ships, but by bypassing hundreds of land-based middlemen and taxing units with his direct trade route, he was able to turn a profit 60 times the cost of his voyage and so whet the appetite of western Europe for more oceanic trade. More and more ships began arriving off the African coast.

Since local settlement patterns kept African traders' interests centered on the rivers, it was European oceangoing vessels that quickly came to dominate the new carrying trade of the western coasts. In the interior, African merchants continued to control both the traditional land and river trades, for Europe was still too weak to drive far inland into Africa, much less to conquer territory. Indeed, so stoutly was the continent defended by both African armies and tropical diseases that it would be 450 years (1450–1900) before the Europeans penetrated most areas of Africa. The forest regions of the coast, moreover, quickly proved a veritable "white man's grave": some 60 percent of the European traders died during their first year in residence, principally from tropical fevers.

Most African rulers welcomed increased international commerce, and although local authorities occasionally had to punish dishonest European merchants by placing an embargo on further commerce until debts or misdeeds were made good, a steady Atlantic trade was soon in operation between the African coastal states and western European middlemen. For most societies bordering the sea this trade spelled amazing new opportunities for wealth. Previously the coastal peoples had been poor relations far from the commercial activity of the continent's great interior empires. The new ocean trade changed all that; the coast was now the cutting edge of commerce, and thus the new foreign trade was avidly welcomed by local rulers.

African rulers rented coastal trading stations to Europeans, who fortified them for protection from cutthroat European competitors. The local rulers did not fear these trading stations because they could cut the European traders off from food, water, and commerce whenever necessary; local middlemen were not worried because African rulers simply refused European traders permission to enter into the interior, where they might become competitors for Africa's domestic trade. Yet the nature of the trade would soon be changed by events far across the western ocean.

Europe's conquest of the Americas had opened up a treasure trove of minerals and vast, fertile agricultural lands—if only the conquerors could find skilled laborers capable of working profitably in the new climate. Initially the white invaders tried to meet their labor needs with Native Americans who had been legally, if immorally, enslaved during the wars of conquest, but when far too many of them succumbed to disease and cruel treatment, it became clear that their enslavement was not a viable long-term policy. White workers were sent out from Europe, but too few Europeans were willing to emigrate as common laborers to the American wilderness, and fewer still—even among those sent unwillingly as bound labor or in punishment for crimes—had the agricultural skills and physical endurance to handle the challenge.

The solution came when the Spanish and other Atlantic European powers found an alternative source of labor at their trading stations on the African coast, where workers who knew both mining and tropical farming could be purchased cheaply and transported for extremely low prices. African slaves proved a bargain in the lower Americas because their labor in the mercantile systems of the New World was worth so much more than it was in tropical Africa, where hoe agriculture produced little in the way of surplus wealth. Moreover, Africans, who were carried by shorter transport routes to the Americas and possessed superior resistance to tropical fevers, died at only one-third the rate of Europeans brought to New World plantations.

Ironically, despite their low cost, suitable abilities, and superior health, African laborers might not have been the only labor choice for New World plantations if capitalism had been further developed toward wage labor or if steamships had been sailing the high seas when the Americas were discovered. After the ending of the Atlantic slave trade in the nineteenth century, contract labor continued to pour into the Caribbean and other ports of the New World, but by that time, when steamships were providing healthier and cheaper long-range oceanic transportation, people from India, China, and nonwestern Europe were preferred for their even lower labor costs. In the economic era before steam, however, Africans quickly became the labor of choice for American development.

The primary source for the millions of slave laborers who would be transported across the Atlantic was West and West Central Africa. Most victims of the slave trade originally lost their freedom after being taken prisoner during African wars. There were no international rules about the treatment of prisoners of war, and enslavement seemed less brutal than many of the alternatives. In places like western Europe at that time it was still considered a captor's right to execute his prisoners if he so desired.

Many other Africans became slaves when they were kidnapped by armed thugs (usually from neighboring territories) who roved the interior trade routes of Africa alongside legitimate merchants. Smaller numbers of people were forced into slavery by traditional legal actions that mandated enslavement to settle debts or as punishment for certain crimes. For the most part, it is fair to say, Africans enslaved not countrymen but enemies, whom they sold away to the foreign traders on the coast.

The vast majority of the new slaves were youths between 10 and 24 years old, just entering the prime of their lives. In composition, 14 percent were children (children made up 30 percent of the African population), 30 percent were young women (who made up around 25 percent of the African population), and 56 percent were young men (also 25 percent of the general population). Among the young adults, twice as many men were transported across the Atlantic as women. American demand rejected older slaves as difficult to train and unlikely to survive, and so men and women over 30 were rarely sold and brought much lower prices. As a result, older adults were seldom kidnapped, and aged captives were either retained on the coast or killed by the raiders at the place of battle.

Far different from the European emigrants, who tended to be from the lower classes, the African slaves exported to America, especially those taken in war, were commonly, as an English observer of the Gambian region observed, "people of distinction, such as princes, priests and persons high in office . . . conducted by Mandingoes in droves of twenty, thirty and forty, chained together."[1] Even African royalty often ended up in slavery; as a result, Africa lost more leadership, and Afro-America gained more, than is commonly realized.

The pricing of the international slave trade was driven as much by local African supply as by foreign demand: since the supplies of African slaves on the coast did not go up and down in direct response to increasing and decreasing Euro-American labor requirements, African traders clearly had agendas of their own. The much greater demand for males in the Americas should have driven up the price for men; instead, women cost more than men on the African coast (twice as much in Senegambia, for example). The higher price for women reflected the decisions of African men in the coastal societies to take advantage of the slave trade by purchasing additional wives, thereby raising the prices.

European and American merchants purchased African slaves for what seemed to them relatively low exchange values in textiles, guns, liquor, metals, and cowrie shell money. But to the African suppliers, the prices appeared remarkably high. Thus, both African and European slave traders raced to make gains in what seemed to them a profitable situation. The potential advantage for West African dealers can be seen when it is realized that in the 1680s a male slave could be legally traded for 17 guns on the western coast; at that time the value of 17 trade muskets was roughly equivalent to six times the yearly cost of living for a common man. Today, in our own world, many a thief will take a man's life for much less.

Deeper into Africa, of course, the original enslaver got less than the coastal trading price when he sold his slaves; indeed, he usually got even less than it would have cost to raise a child to an age equivalent to that of the young person he was selling. Why then did merchants engage in the slave trade, since the continent was losing value with each person sold away? Part of the answer is that the continent was not doing the trading.

For the original enslavers, who were taking human beings through war or kidnapping, slaves seemed almost like free goods. The slave dealers profited on their deals; it was the societies losing members that were being injured, but they had no say in the exchange. Thus, the private wealth of certain powerful African elites increased at the same time that the public wealth in human capital of certain African societies was declining. It is a familiar problem, in other guises, in our own era.

One victim of the slave trade who later came to reflect on its causes blamed the greed of whites and blacks alike. Olaudah Equiano was kidnapped as a child by African traders before eventually being sold to Europeans on the coast.

> From what I can recollect of [the battles between African states] they appear to have been eruptions of one little state or district on the other, to obtain prisoners or booty. Perhaps they were incited to this, by those traders who brought the European goods . . . amongst us. Such a mode of obtaining slaves in Africa is common; and I believe more are procured this way, and by kidnapping, than any other. When a trader wants slaves, he applies to a chief for them, and tempts him with his wares. It is not extraordinary if on this occasion he yields to the temptation with as little firmness, and accepts the prices of his fellow creature's liberty, with as little reluctance as the enlightened merchant.—Accordingly he falls on his neighbors, and a desperate battle ensues. If he prevails and takes prisoners, he gratifies his avarice by selling them.[2]

From the perspective of those Africans who traded in slaves, the people they sold away were not countrymen but outsiders—prisoners of war, criminals, or kidnap victims from other societies. Thus, selling them was not considered immoral; instead, it seemed both reasonable and profitable. Moreover, bartering for the provisions white slavers needed for the Atlantic crossing brought the coastal elite an additional 50 percent in profits. All in all, for those on the coast, selling foreigners was a lucrative business.

For Africa as a whole, however, the economics were much different. For the continent the profitability of the slave trade was canceled out by the high costs of increasing warfare, the social insecurity caused by slave raiding, and the loss of so many young productive people. Moreover, the small upper class who gained from the trade too often frittered away much of their new wealth on imported luxury goods; there was little domestic investment of the kind that would bring productive new growth to the continent. Caught between economic stages of development, Africa gained little from the private economic decisions of its coastal elite; in that sense, being on the periphery of the expanding capitalist world proved as injurious for Africa as it did for those shipped away from the continent to the Americas.

We must remember that most of the negative results of the slave trade either were invisible on the coast or would not show up until later. Since the coastal lands had traditionally been among the most poorly developed regions of sub-Saharan Africa, when new trading opportunities arose, the local peoples saw the commerce as a heaven-sent opportunity to increase their wealth and power. As a result, the era of the slave trade was marked by great increases in the size and influence of Africa's western coastal states, while at the same time greater use of new American food crops was increasing the population growth rate and thus disguising the negative demographic effects of exporting people.

Since the coastal peoples did not organize their world in racial categories, they saw no immorality in selling foreign African slaves to white Europeans. Indeed, early on the trade was often considered a necessity to finance defense spending, since the lucrative international commerce with Europe led to increasing conflicts between the African coastal states struggling to dominate the new trade. Since the winners became rich and the losers enslaved, the battles set off a series of costly arms races: by 1730 some 180,000 muskets a year were entering West Africa from the coast, and by 1800 over 500,000 weapons were imported yearly.

Africa was not yet dependent on Europe. Indeed, things seemed to be going well: the coastal states were growing in size and influence, their elites were becoming vastly wealthier, and cheap foreign imports such as East Indian textiles were improving the material standard of living of the common people. African states were trading what they considered excess and dangerous population for foreign luxuries, cheap textiles, tools, metals, bargain-priced cowrie money, and guns. Although the majority of women and children taken in slavery were not sent abroad but were incorporated into coastal societies, the excess men were usually sold overseas. This sexual imbalance led to coastal societies becoming increasingly polygynous and densely populated, while the smaller interior states were seriously weakened.

Unfortunately, as the Atlantic slave trade increased, so, too, did the numbers of people held in indigenous forms of African servitude, which were becoming less and less protective of human rights. Africa, like the New World, was inevitably being corrupted by the moral cost of large-scale commerce in human beings. Indeed, by 1770 there were probably as many slaves in West and West Central Africa as in all the countries of the Americas—approximately 2.5 million people were in African bondage.

Most coastal kings were pleased with the commerce, which had made them richer and more powerful than they had ever been. Unfortunately, as the Dahomean ruler Agaja Trudo came to discover when he tried to end the corrupting slave trade in his region, the world market, not the African merchant, was setting the basic terms of the exchange. Thus, if Dahomey wanted foreign imports, the Dahomeans had to sell people or business and weapons would flow in dangerously high amounts to their enemies.

In retrospect, we can see that the Atlantic slave trade was not as beneficial a commerce as it first appeared from the African traders' perspective. It vastly increased African domestic slavery but not African labor efficiency;

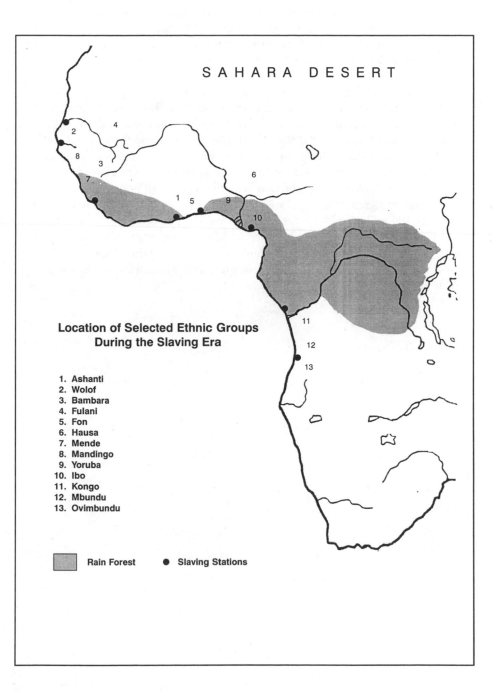

SAHARA DESERT

**Location of Selected Ethnic Groups
During the Slaving Era**

1. Ashanti
2. Wolof
3. Bambara
4. Fulani
5. Fon
6. Hausa
7. Mende
8. Mandingo
9. Yoruba
10. Ibo
11. Kongo
12. Mbundu
13. Ovimbundu

Rain Forest   ● Slaving Stations

moreover, imported luxuries did nothing for Africa's productive development. In fact, cheap foreign textiles undercut local producers. In those rare areas where Europeans were able to force an entry into Africa—the east coast Swahili city-states and the Kongo region in Central Africa—they proved incompetent to hold the trading networks together, and these old centers of power fell into poverty much as did the former Inca and Aztec empires in America.

All told, Africa sent nearly 12 million of her sons and daughters westward to the Americas in the years between 1500 and 1900. It is worth noting that this number roughly parallels the nearly 12 million who were sent eastward and northward across the Sahara Desert, the Red Sea, and the Indian Ocean by Arab slave traders during the longer period of 650–1900. Some scholars have speculated that the result of these forced human emigrations from the continent may have been a reduction in Africa's potential population growth: the continent's estimated population of 50 million in 1850 might have been closer to 100 million without the international slave trades.

In return for the Atlantic commerce, Africa grew materially richer, and many of its coastal states grew far more powerful. As Africa grew wealthier, however, it lost human capital and thus grew less self-sufficient and dangerously more dependent on foreign trade.

five

The Middle Passage and Beyond

Jesús, Estella, Esperanza, Mercy:
Sails flashing to the wind like weapons,
sharks following the moans the fever and the dying;
horror the corposant and compass rose.
Middle Passage:
voyage through death
to life upon these shores

The African American poet Robert Hayden, "Middle Passage,"
Selected Poems (1966)

The process of enslavement, transport, and seasoning was a passage through hell that carried a terrible price in suffering and death. The horror had begun in Africa with wars and small-scale raiding during which nearly as many people died as were finally enslaved. Only a minority of those taken captive or kidnapped were destined to be sold away from the continent, but that minority was unlucky enough to experience African slavery at its worst—which was bad enough that very few Africans who gained their freedom in America ever tried to make their way home. Of those new slaves shipped to the African coast, nearly one in five died of disease or mistreatment along the way or in the barracoons awaiting departure. To return to such a situation was for most of those who experienced it unthinkable.

Among the 12 million Africans who survived to be placed aboard the ships of the foreign slave traders, conditions got no better. Somewhere between one in five and one in ten of all the people put on board would die crossing the ocean during the deadly Middle Passage. Imagine a modern airline trip on which an average of one passenger in every row dies before the plane lands, their bodies unceremoniously dumped out of the rear of the plane along the way.

Even arrival on American shores did not bring a halt to the slaughter: one of every four who had been strong enough to make it across the Atlantic would die during the first several years of American "seasoning," as adjusting to the new environment was called. In total, then, nearly one in every three of the original captives taken in Africa died from the process of enslavement.

Such an immense loss of life would not have made any economic sense if the native population of the Americas had not been expiring even more rapidly. The wars and cultural shocks that followed the European invasion of the late fifteenth and early sixteenth centuries, combined with the onslaught of Old World diseases for which Native Americans had no immunities, threatened to all but destroy the original peoples. In those early years Europeans were not willing to emigrate in numbers anywhere near sufficient to replace the native labor force; those Europeans who did come to the Americas too often quickly died. Indeed, Europeans, when they were put to work in tropical conditions—in the West Indies, for example—died off at six times the rate they would have in Europe and at three times the rate of black workers.

The imperial nations of Europe had found their answer to the labor problems of the Americas in West Africa, where black laborers could be purchased both easily and relatively cheaply. Although carrying Africans as slaves across the Atlantic Ocean always remained a chancy enterprise, and earnings varied considerably from place to place and voyage to voyage, profits usually ran somewhere between 25 and 50 percent. The result was an important and profitable business—but a brutal and inhumane one.

It is hard to imagine how soul-testing the passage from African freedom to American slavery must have been for those who experienced it. First there was the trauma of capture during war or by kidnappers. Then came a trip to the coast that was usually as physically exhausting as it was cruel; the traders who specialized in bringing slaves to coastal barracoons and river stations tried to move their captives as quickly and cheaply as possible before illness or escape could lessen their profits. Comfort and kind treatment were not part of the equation.

Psychologically the last days in the barracoons of Africa took captives a considerable distance along the brutal passage from freedom to chattel slavery. Days of cramped waiting, often in the cellars of the stifling hot slaving stations (called factories in those days), must have dragged by, sweat drop by sweat drop, in endless boredom. Even worse, when depression lifted enough for conversations to begin, talk too often revolved around rumors that the prisoners were to be sold to hideously repulsive foreigners who were going to carry their victims off to the lands of cannibal death far across the western sea. Even those new slaves long since reduced to vacant stares must have groaned in dismay when, as in a fevered dream, the fearsome aliens materialized in large ocean-going vessels gliding silently into view, their masts towering heavenward and rigged like monstrous cannibal fetish shrines.

Mohamommah Gardo Baquaqua described the terror of that irrevocable moment: "I had never seen a ship before, and my idea of it was, that it was some object of worship of the white man. I imagined that we were all to be slaughtered."[1] To Belinda, a young slave woman, the alien appearance of white men, "whose faces were like the moon and whose bows and arrows were like the thunder and lightning," seemed to be visual proof of their evil magic and horrible ways.[2]

"I was now persuaded that I had gotten into a world of bad spirits and that they were going to kill me," recalled Olaudah Equiano. Coming on deck to see desolate blacks chained next to a great copper boiling pot convinced the young boy that he was "to be eaten by those white men with horrible looks, red faces, and loose hair," who barked their orders so cruelly in an alien tongue.[3]

In the tropical heat the stench of the ship and its unwashed crew was overpowering. Chained below in the darkness, the new slaves could feel the departing vessel begin its slow rolling, creaking morbidly with every invisible swell. Most must have longed to give up the ghost; those weakened by illness moaned pitifully, while others cried out in fear or railed angrily against their fate. Often it was not long before the seas became heavier and the wretching sounds of sea sickness would fill the dark hold.

After that, no matter how often the necessary tubs were emptied or the hold was washed down with seawater and vinegar, below deck it would continue to reek of sweat, vomit, and the putrid human wastes that had sloshed back and forth when the hatches were battened down. Certainly some voyages were better than others; if the new slaves stayed healthy, if the seas were light and the winds brisk, and if the crew was more humane than usual, it might have seemed tolerable. Too often, though, captives found the conditions unbearable. Some rapidly died of illnesses that in other circumstances they would have survived. Others tried to kill themselves by jumping overboard or refusing to eat.

Slavers tried to reduce the likelihood of Africans making suicidal leaps into the sea by rigging nets along the sides of the ship. If slaves still reached the water, crewmen were sent after them so that an example could be made; such would-be suicides were, ironically enough, executed. Afterward their bodies would be mutilated, for the slavers were convinced that Africans believed mutilation would end the cycle of rebirth that otherwise carried a suicide back home to his family.

When other slaves, out of depression, illness, or suicidal intent, chose not to eat, the crewmen would use hot coals to sear open their lips or force funnels into their mouths to pour food down their throats. To those who feared cannibalism, the white crewmen's actions seemed strong evidence that they were fattening their captives for the kill.

Despite the slavers' torturous attempts to keep their human cargo alive, on most voyages there were men and women whose desire for freedom and release led them to suicide or a willful death. Since these victims of the Middle

Passage believed they would return to their former African homelands in the next life, their deaths mark one of the world's greatest, but most overlooked, religious martyrdoms.

Because the conditions of the Middle Passage were so terrible, the slavers often faced battles to the death during uprisings by the prisoners held aboard ship. John Newton, a reformed slave trader, explained both the extreme dangers and the measures slavers took to reduce the likelihood of such revolts in *Thoughts upon the Africa Slave Trade*, published in 1788:

> Usually about two-thirds of a cargo of slaves are males. When a hundred and fifty or two hundred stout men, torn from their native land, many of whom never saw the sea, much less a ship, till a short space before they had embarked; who have, probably, the same natural prejudice against a white man, as we have against a black; and who often bring with them an apprehension they are bought to be eaten: I say, when thus circumstanced, it is not to be expected that they will tamely resign themselves to their situation. It is taken for granted, that they will attempt to gain their liberty if possible. Accordingly, we dare not trust them, we receive them on board from the first as enemies.[4]

Thus, slaves were often put in irons until the ship was at sea. Later each man was fettered hand and foot to a fellow victim so that movement became possible but only with great teamwork and deliberation. When the men were brought on deck to exercise, chains were commonly run through the irons of each pair so that escape and insurrection became extremely difficult.

The women and children were kept separately and were often free of chains and irons, but far too often they were at the mercy of vicious seamen who had perhaps the worst jobs and dispositions in all Christendom. On the loading of the slaves, the sorry and savage dregs of humanity who served as crew for the slave ships (and who often would not survive the voyage) would stand on deck rudely calling out their foulest thoughts as the women passed before them naked, shivering, and terrified. John Newton recalled the scene: "The poor [black women] cannot understand the language they hear, but the looks and manner of the [crewmen] are sufficiently intelligible. In imagination, the prey is divided, upon the spot, and only reserved til opportunity offers."[5]

It is not surprising that the Africans looked for any opportunity to rise up and strike back against such vile treatment. John Newton understood such insurrections for what they were—noble struggles for liberty or death: "An attempt to rise upon the ship's company, brings on instantaneous and horrid war; for, when they are once in motion, they are desperate. . . . Sometimes when the slaves are ripe for an insurrection, one of them will impeach the affair. . . . The traitor to the cause of liberty is caressed, rewarded, and deemed an honest fellow. The patriots, who formed and animated the plan, if they can be found out, must be treated as villains, and punished, to intimidate the rest."[6]

Parenthetically we should note that Newton captured one of the basic themes of the colonial era, the struggle for freedom, but from a perspective we seldom encounter. Historians have commonly given far too much honor to the Founding Fathers, who were in reality traitors to the principles of freedom, and missed altogether the greater heroism of those black men and women who were a truer vanguard of liberty.

Despite all the precautions of chains, guards, and vicious punishments, revolts remained common on the slave ships. There was an uprising every year or so on French slavers, about one in every 15 voyages; British ships had fewer revolts, but one every other year was common enough. On the smaller vessels that American slavers used there were often several years between uprisings; fewer than 2 percent of the voyages reported revolts.

Few of the Africans successfully carried across the Atlantic were delivered to the English colonies of North America. Brazil took eight times more slaves than did the North American colonies, some 40 percent of the total exported from Africa; the islands of the Caribbean and the settlements of the Guianas between them took another 50 percent. From the perspective of the Atlantic traders, the more distant North America was almost an afterthought; Englishmen in the mainland colonies purchased only about 5 percent of the Africans who were transported from the coast.

In the Caribbean the profits made off a new slave in his first year of bondage paid back the entire cost of the original investment. It is no wonder that conditions remained so harsh in the islands, that six slaves died there for every slave child born: it was cheaper to work a slave to death and purchase a replacement than it was to pay for proper human maintenance and upkeep.

In North America, where the crops slaves produced had less value and higher production costs, it took much longer to earn back the original purchase investment in a slave; therefore, bondspeople were generally better treated. A healthier climate may have been equally important in boosting the North American survival rate. Whatever the cause, blacks died in the English colonies at no worse a rate than whites.

But did physical survival come at the price of cultural death? There is no easy answer to this vexing question. Non-English immigrants from Europe quickly assumed British ways during the colonial era even when they were not enslaved, and contemporary Africans have eagerly adopted American lifestyles without coercion. Living culture is never static. The early Africans who improvised their way into African American life should be as respected for their accomplishments, which shaped all our lives, as pitied for how much they unwillingly lost. The new lives of these Africans varied considerably across time and from region to region, not to mention from slave to slave; to understand what happened we must look into the specific circumstances of a variety of smaller communities in the different colonial regions.

Part Two

Black Life in the Non-English Borderlands

six

The Spanish Territories

[Francisco Menéndez] distinguished himself in the establish-
ment, and cultivation of Mose [North America's first black
town], to improve that settlement, doing all he could so that the
rest of his subjects following his example, would apply themselves to work and learn good customs.

Governor Manuel de Montiano, on Captain Menéndez, leader
of the Mose black militia, 1740

Colonial histories that focus on the political development of the United
States usually disregard the Spanish expeditions and settlements along the
southern and southwestern borders. But in African American history, the
Spanish ventures are too important a part of the early black experience in
North America to be overlooked. Africans and Afro-Spaniards served in a
variety of roles during the sixteenth-century exploring expeditions, and men
and women of mixed Afro-Indian blood were a significant component of early
Spanish settlement right up through the eighteenth century.

As early as the sixteenth century, small numbers of Africans broke away
from early Spanish exploring parties to live with nearby Native American
peoples. These Africans, the first North American colonials to strike out in
pursuit of personal liberty, were also the first Old World immigrants to settle
within our national borders—in areas within the boundaries of present-day
South Carolina, Alabama, Georgia, New Mexico, and Kansas.

Many of the blacks who first reached North America with the Spanish
were *ladinos*, African men and women enslaved during the wars that liberated
Iberia from the Moors. Usually they had been acculturated for a number of
years in the ways of Spain before they were sent west to the Americas. Quite

a few were experienced campaigners who provided much of the logistical support for Spanish ventures such as Ponce de León's Florida expedition of 1513. Their important work as personal servants, craftspeople, musicians, and common laborers has been undervalued by historians of the Spanish borderlands, but the absolute need for their labor and the practical usefulness of their skills were well understood by the Spanish governments of the time and the men who led the exploring campaigns.

When a large Spanish expedition of some six ships and 600 people under Lucas Vázquez de Ayllón arrived along the coast of what is now South Carolina in 1526, included in the company were as many as 100 blacks. Once on land, the expedition moved slowly southward, and when marshy soil, bad weather, inadequate food, and increasing sickness exacerbated a succession crisis in the company's leadership, the blacks came into their own. Some of the African slaves rose in a countercoup against the new commander, Ginés Doncel, who had illegally taken control of the exploring party after the original commander's death from illness. Doncel wanted to abandon the new colony immediately; apparently some of the blacks disagreed. In setting fire to one of his huts, they opened a rebellion and wrote the first chapter of colonial resistance to tyranny in North America.

After a short battle, a more popular group among the Spaniards gained the upper hand, and the battered exploring party quickly retreated away from what is now the Georgia coast to Santo Domingo. Many of the blacks, however, are said to have stayed behind to live with the local Guale Indians. These Africans were the first non-Indian immigrants into the lands that would become the United States, although the society they joined was a Native American one.

Several years later the most famous of the early African-Spanish adventurers to explore North America arrived, a dark-skinned Moroccan called Estevanico, originally from Azamor on the west coast of Morocco. Estevanico landed in Florida as one of the Africans assigned to the ill-fated Pánfilo de Narváez expedition of 1528. When that venture was destroyed by disease and Indian resistance, Estevanico was among the few left alive to be taken into Indian captivity. After several years of enslavement to the native people of the region, the last four Narváez survivors planned an escape westward across the lower Gulf Coast to Mexico.

Nominally Estevanico was still a servant to his master, but in fact, Estevanico's talents as a healer and as the group's chief linguist, diplomat, and guide helped the small party to endure their desperate flight through hostile territory and eventually reach safety in Spanish-controlled Mexico. As Alvar Núñez Cabeza de Vaca explained: "The Negro [Estevanico] was in constant conversation; he informed himself about the ways we wished to take, of the towns there were, and the matters we desired to know."[1] Estevanico's competence and loyalty during this long overland ordeal earned him considerable respect among the Spanish; the fantastic stories he reported about a land of gold in the interior of North America were thus taken very seriously.

European myths, Indian exaggerations, and the recently looted riches of Mexico and Peru doubtless inspired Estevanico's and his companions' interest in the golden treasures supposedly to be discovered somewhere deeper in North America. Estevanico at once tried to persuade Spanish officials to undertake a new exploration into the desertlike interior lands to the north—present-day Arizona and New Mexico. Was it only coincidence that, within 40 years of Estevanico's expedition to the mythical seven golden cities of Cibola, a similar but far better equipped Moroccan venture was sent southward across the Sahara to conquer the golden lands of the African interior? It is likely that the dreams of Europe and Africa blended in Estevanico's mind with the North African tales he had heard about the fabled wealth of the African Sudan to create one of the first golden visions of America's future.

Because of his reports and proven skills, Estevanico was assigned in 1539 to discover the route and then guide Father Marcos de Niza to the reportedly golden cities of Cibola. To facilitate his passage among the native peoples, Estevanico dressed as a great medicine man with bells and feathers on his arms and legs. He had learned that he would be more impressive to the Indians if he carried a symbol of his magical powers; thus, as he proceeded northward, he conspicuously displayed a large gourd decorated with strings of bells and a red and white feather. He quickly attracted a large native entourage of several hundred followers, some of whom, unfortunately, may have been enemies of the people he sought to visit. Whatever the case, his procession clearly seemed dangerous to the Pueblo Indians he was approaching, for they took him captive and, before he could discover that the golden cities he sought were just a myth, apparently killed him.

Still, it is important to note that before any white man, Spanish or otherwise, explored the territories that would become Arizona and New Mexico, Estevanico was there blazing a trail. Moreover, he and the later Afro-Mexicans made such an impression on the territory's Pueblo Indians that, according to Zuni legend, his whole expedition was made up of "Black Mexicans" and Sono-li Indians; as the Pueblo remembered it, the troops who returned to enslave the Zuni people in punishment for his death were likewise Black Mexicans, not white Spaniards.

Estevanico was only the first of many Africans who would enter the Spanish Southwest during the colonial era. There were blacks on both of the immediate follow-up expeditions quickly sent out in 1540 to exploit the riches hinted at in Estevanico's reports. One Negro in Hernando de Alarcón's exploring party was the only man brave enough (or perhaps knowledgeable enough) to cross the desert to pass on word of Alarcón's dangerous proximity to Francisco Vázquez de Coronado's companion expedition. But more important to history, when the rest of the party returned home, three of the blacks among Coronado's company stayed behind as pioneering settlers in the village of Cicuye, southeast of Santa Fe.

When far to the east Hernando de Soto tried an alternative route into what was hoped would be the golden interior of America, his expedition also depended upon Africans, mostly as part of the supply train. Several among them in 1540 effected the escape of a noble Indian woman of the Carolina Cofitachiqui (*or* Cufitatchiqui) whom de Soto had taken hostage. One of the black men, a slave of Andre de Vasconcelos de Silva, was said to have become the noble lady's lover before her rescue; both he and an Afro-Spaniard companion named Gómez reportedly left the expedition to marry native women, subsequently settling among the local Indians.

Was it significant that this incident took place in the same territory that had given harbor to the escaped black slaves of Ayllón's expedition 14 years earlier? The great Cofitachiqui lady must have known of Ayllón's exploration; de Soto's men found Spanish axes and trade items in a local grave. The appearance of Africans in the party may therefore have had a significance to the noblewoman unsuspected by the Spanish.

Interestingly, in 1653 an Englishman exploring Carolina from the north was taken to a Tuscarora Indian village where a rich Spaniard was in residence with his "family" (or entourage?) of 30, including 7 Negroes; also present in the village was a historically mysterious black resident said to be of a great nation called the "Newxes."

De Soto's expedition lost other black slaves who deserted or were left behind to live with the Indians. A Negro named John Biscayan later deserted to join the Coças Indians, and another black man named Robles, who was too ill to go on, was left behind and lived some dozen years at Tascalua, according to follow-up reports of the Don Tristan de Luna y Arellano expedition of 1559–61.

Once the exploring years were over, black and mixed-race servants and slaves became even more important during the early settlement of the Spanish borderlands. Afro-Mexicans, for example, were numerous among the colonists Juan de Oñate led northward into New Mexico in 1598.

Unlike their later experience with the English of being held in a castelike condition, blacks in the early Southwest usually either blended into Spanish Creole society or married Indians, thereby becoming effectively Indian, since inheritance among most Native Americans passed through the woman's line. This process of dual assimilation was well under way when civil war broke out in New Mexico in 1640–43; mulattoes and *sambahigos* (sons of Indian men and Negroes) were among the troops involved in the fighting.

When growing resentment led the Pueblo Indians of New Mexico to rebel against Spanish rule in 1680, people with partial African ancestry were on both sides of the conflict. The most important of these southwestern African Americans was a Pueblo named Domingo Navanjo, the son of a black settler and an Indian woman. Interestingly, Navanjo, a key resistance leader of the Pueblo, portrayed himself as the representative of a mythical black sun spirit—thereby combining his racial heritage with traditional Pueblo religious ideas about spirit maskers and Spanish claims of divinity made during their expeditions from Mexico. When the revolt proved successful, blacks who identified with the Spanish were forced temporarily to retreat southward, while the Afro-Indian Navanjo became a legendary Pueblo hero.

When the Spanish returned in 1692 to reassert their control, still more blacks entered the region with the invading army. Typical of the many Negroes who served in the era's Spanish colonial armies was Sabastián Rodríguez, an African from San Pablo de Luanda in Angola, who served as a drummer among the troops. In fact, African expertise in percussion instruments made African drummers throughout the colonial era valued among all military organizations. In the seventeenth century men of mixed African and Spanish blood had the bearing and skills to be frequently utilized as majordomos in the Spanish missions of the Southwest, for contrary to later stereotypes, far more African than European Americans were men of upper-class upbringing.

The importance of the African American population of the territories that now make up the American Southwest is indicated in the extremely conservative estimate that at the end of the eighteenth century at least one out of every 20 people living in the colonial-era Spanish borderlands of Texas, New Mexico, Arizona, and California could be characterized in U.S. racial terminology as African American.[2] In the late eighteenth century the majority of the troops along the northern Texas frontier were either blacks or mulattoes. Conditions further west were much the same, and the mixed-race Afro-Mexicans called *coyotes*, who dominated the labor force of the northwestern Mexican province of Sonora, would soon move north.

Thus, it should not be surprising that numerous Afro-Mexicans were among the soldiers and settlers moving into Alta California in the late eighteenth century, so much so that at least one-fifth, and probably more, of the founding Hispano-Californians of that era could trace a recent African ancestry. Settlers of pure and mixed African blood were among the workers who built the early California missions and helped found the villages of San Diego in 1769 and Los Angeles in 1781.

Some of these Africans were highly skilled, like the slave named Moreno who served as Father Junipero Serra's linguist during Indian negotiations; more important, it was Moreno who was in charge of carrying the first Old World plants and seeds into California to establish an agricultural base for the settlements. By 1790 persons of mixed ancestry owned vast tracts of southern California—among them, Maria Rita Valdez, who owned the Rancho lands now known as Beverly Hills, and Francisco Reyes, who controlled the entire San Fernando Valley. According to the 1790 census, 15 percent of the San Francisco population was African, as was 25 percent of San Jose, 19 percent of Santa Barbara, and 23 percent of Los Angeles; many more Californians were of mixed blood.

Blacks were also important along the Spanish frontier of the eastern seaboard, where the Spanish used Africans for the hard labor of clearing land and planting crops as well as to build fortifications and other structures. African Americans who arrived as slaves with the Spanish had been living in Saint Augustine since its settlement in 1565, although many others had escaped to join the local Aís Indians, among whom lived a shipwrecked mulatto named Luis, perhaps encouraging the runaways. Blacks from the Saint Augustine settlement were also sent northward several times in the late sixteenth century to build and repair fortifications for a Spanish post at Elena (now Parris Island, South Carolina). All of this took place many years before the first blacks arrived in Virginia or the *Mayflower* landed with English colonists in Massachusetts.

By 1683 the black population of Saint Augustine was important enough that the town formed a black militia regiment, which joined in the Spanish raids against English Carolina in 1686. The result was that Spanish Florida, with its free black population and black troops, became an ever more frightening specter to nearby English slaveholders and, at the same time, a magnet of freedom to African American slaves from the southernmost colonies. Enough slaves were successful in escaping southward to Spanish Florida or to Florida Indian tribes that in 1688, and again in 1726, envoys from South Carolina were sent to Saint Augustine to negotiate for their return. The Spanish refused to hand over the former slaves on the grounds they had married local black citizens and converted to Catholicism since their arrival in the settlement.

In addition to the self-liberated slaves who came to Florida on their own, English-owned slaves were often carried south against their will, kidnapped by raiding parties of Indians or free Afro-Hispanics living in Spanish Florida. Unfortunately, these kidnap victims, like many of the runaways, often were not liberated upon reaching Florida's Spanish settlements; instead, they were taken up and resold into Caribbean bondage by unscrupulous Spanish officials. In theory, Spanish authorities should have offered sanctuary to any escaped slaves who sought baptism with the intention of converting to Catholicism, but even when sanctuary was offered, protection did not always mean freedom.

So it was for many former slaves of the English who had escaped to the Yamassee Indians during their war with the English forces in Carolina, only to find themselves reenslaved once they reached Florida. Their leader, an African of Mandingo ethnicity who took the name Francisco Menéndez in Saint Augustine, soon became informed about Spanish law and began a long struggle by petition to win recognition of his group's freedom from the Spanish crown. Meanwhile, Spanish authorities recognized Menéndez's abilities by appointing him commander of the local slave militia in 1726. After Menéndez's black troops helped defend Saint Augustine from British attack in 1728, the crown commended their valor, and a new governor finally granted them freedom in 1738. This was wise policy, since black troops were crucial to the Spanish military effort in Florida, serving as scouts and cavalrymen as well as crewmen for local patrol boats.

All this black advancement was only more worrisome to the authorities in English Carolina, and when diplomacy failed to stop the leakage of English-owned slaves southward, military measures were undertaken. In 1740, during the War of Jenkins' Ear, Gov. James E. Oglethorpe of Georgia invaded the eastern Florida territories and captured several towns, including the Pueblo de Gracia Real de Santa Teresa de Mose, known as Mose (*pronounced* Mo-say), a stone-walled village built two years previously by 100 free blacks and their families—including Indian spouses—two miles north of Saint Augustine, under the leadership of Captain Menéndez.

Mose seems to have been the first black town in North America; most of its settlers came originally as escaped slaves from English Carolina, although they had mostly been born in West Africa. The housing was probably built in the African style of their youth: the Spanish noted that the roofs of the small dwellings were thatched like Indian huts, and the use in the fortification of packed earth, ditches, prickly plants, and a lookout platform was probably based on African precedents as much as on European or Native American examples.

When the Oglethorpe expedition ground to a halt after its siege of Saint Augustine failed, the Spanish—including a mulatto regiment and the black troops of the Mose militia—counterattacked, and the blacks liberated the region's first African American village from foreign control.

It would not be the last time during the colonial period when African Americans would find themselves carrying the banner of liberty against English colonists. Despite a national mythology that portrays the English settlers of North America as harbingers of individual liberty, in this case and many others the colonial English were actually the supporters of enslavement against a variety of African American efforts to increase or maintain liberty.

The Spanish later ceded the Florida territory to the British at the end of the Seven Years' War in 1763, and the Spanish and Afro-Spaniards living there pulled out and resettled in Havana. Still, during the next 20 years of British rule new slaves from Africa, South Carolina, and Georgia were imported into Florida to work local rice, indigo, cotton, and sugar plantations, and blacks soon outnumbered whites there by a factor of two to one.

When the British relinquished their claims in eastern Florida in 1784 as part of the peace process that ended the American Revolution, returning that territory to Spain, some 7,000 whites and 10,000 blacks lived in the region. Although most of the African Americans there were enslaved, they were the majority population of the region and should be recognized as the primary settler group in late colonial English Florida.[3]

From the Spanish perspective, Florida may have been lost in 1763 after the Seven Years' War, but in the process the Louisiana territory had been gained from the French. The Spanish quickly began to build up their new holdings by increasing the importation of slaves from the African regions of Senegambia, the Bight of Benin, the Bight of Biafra, and Central Africa, the largest number being imported during the decade 1777–87.

With the threat of insurrection posed by so many new slaves compounded by an old guard of hostile French planters, Spanish officials looked to the colony's free blacks as necessary allies. To win African American support, the Spanish gave free blacks special exemptions from civil penalties and taxes in exchange for militia service and other duties, such as maintaining levees, fighting fires, and hunting fugitive slaves.

While the Spanish might have wanted to assert stronger controls—they paid less attention to keeping slave families together than did the French, for example—conditions in the colony forced them to tread lightly: many of the slaves near the coast were armed, and running away to English-controlled territory was relatively easy for slaves during the disorders of the Revolutionary War.

Louisiana was also a black-majority area at the end of the colonial era: the census of 1778 showed that over half of its nearly 40,000 people were slaves.[4]

seven

The French Borderlands

> The inhabitants of America in general, French as well as
> English, do not part with their blacks unless they know them to
> be bad or vicious. . . . If one wishes to follow what is practiced
> among the English, French ships must bring blacks to Louisiana
> and the settlers of this colony must be able to pay for them
> either in kind or in money.
>
> The French Ministry of Colonies, answering a request from
> Governor Bienville to open a slave trade to Louisiana (1708)

As had been the case on the Spanish frontier, new Africans and African
Americans became an extremely important force in the French settlements of
Louisiana, both in the development of local culture and in supplying crucial
labor skills. Starting in 1699, the colony's leadership pleaded with the French
king to send slaves from Africa; officials believed that neither Indian slaves nor
white indentured servants would be able to provide a satisfactory labor force
in Louisiana's hot climate. Two decades later, in 1719, the first two slave ships
arrived at the mouth of the Mississippi with their precious cargo. So popular
was the importation of African labor that by 1727 African-born blacks had
become the majority population among the settlers; blacks would remain predominant numerically among the settlers of Louisiana until the French ceded
their Louisiana settlements to Spain in 1763.[1]

The historian Gwendolyn Midlo Hall has demonstrated that most of these
early black Louisianians were imported as slaves from the Senegambia region
of the West African coast, and over half of them—some 3,250 out of 5,987—
arrived during the five years from 1726 to 1731. They had been sought out
precisely for their skills as rice-growers, cattle-keepers, and metalworkers.
And as we shall see was the case in early South Carolina, it was the West

45

African knowledge of rice agriculture, indigo manufacture, and cattle-keeping that made both colonies initially successful. Additional blacks were brought in from the West Indian colony of Saint Domingue to develop a sugar crop in the new Louisiana territory. Although Africans were not the political and social leaders of Louisiana, it was their practical knowledge that made the colony productive, and their sweat that generated the bulk of the profits.

Much as had been the case in the Spanish settlements, Louisiana authorities used slaves as the backbone of the construction battalions building the original fortifications and serving in the colonial militia. A pioneering vanguard of black workers built and improved area roads, cut back trees, cleared fields for planting, built levees and irrigation works, and unloaded all the necessary supplies from the ships they rowed upriver; only then were the planters able to move out onto the land, the precursors of the great Louisiana slave plantations that would bring riches to the Gulf Coast.

As in Florida, some of the African slaves brought to the colony escaped their bondage by joining the local Indians, with whom they fought as allies against the growing encroachment of the Europeans. Among the Indians, escaped Africans had the freedom to hunt and cultivate when they felt like it rather than in answer to someone's command. Moreover, Indian women made attractive sexual partners for the many single African men, who outnumbered black women in the colony two to one. The children of these Afro-Indian unions were called *grifs*, and they would later become a distinctive and important subgroup of Louisiana's African American population.

Precisely because Indians and blacks both had reasons to dislike the French, their rapid intermixing frightened French authorities, who therefore placed a high priority on sowing distrust between the potential allies. As Gov. Étienne de Périer explained in 1731: "The greatest misfortune which could befall the colony and which would inevitably lead to its total loss would be a union between the Indian nations and the black slaves, but happily there has always been a great aversion between them . . . and we take great care to maintain it."[2]

Despite the harsh living conditions of frontier slavery, the black population of Louisiana grew rapidly from its own natural increase; in the merger of African cultures within the milieu of the Indian and French border, a unique way of speaking developed, the antecedent of what is now known as Louisiana Creole. The vocabulary was primarily French in origin, but the grammatical structure remained largely African. In a similar way, many of the specialized terms used in hunting and fishing the swampy bayous came from African languages and have survived right up to the present day.

One significant difference between the African American experience in French Louisiana and elsewhere in the English, or even Spanish, colonies was the greater tendency of French colonists to absorb free people of African descent, and especially those of mixed African-European ancestry, within the white population. In theory, the French also supported a more humane form of bondage—Governor Beinville's slave code, for example, invalidated sales that separated husbands and wives, or children under 14 from their parents—but it is not clear how many settlers actually followed the rules.

Certainly for most African Americans, conditions were difficult in Louisiana. As was typical elsewhere, laws limited the opportunities for blacks to engage in business, accumulate property, assemble at night, or even leave their residences without a pass. For habitual runaways among the bondspeople, brutal punishments like ear cropping, branding, and hamstringing were prescribed and often carried out.

The lands that made up French Louisiana during the colonial period were far more extensive than just the territory around New Orleans and the lower Mississippi Delta. Louisiana Africans were also imported upriver in relatively large numbers to provide the labor necessary to develop the fertile Natchez region, which was then called Upper Mississippi. This territory was initially occupied by the French in 1716, and a decade later over one-third of the population was African.[3] Natchez slaves not only produced tobacco, indigo, rice, cotton, and wheat but developed a timber industry, cut and dressed logs, and produced tar and pitch for export. These Upper Mississippi settlements prospered until a destructive war with the Natchez Indians in 1729 soured the French on the region and convinced them that the fearful possibility of a dangerous African-Indian alliance developing was too great to continue large-scale operations in the area.

The Natchez War led the French to make a concerted policy of more tightly binding all the colony's blacks to the settler side. To secure African loyalty, slaves were offered freedom in exchange for military service, and blacks both bonded and free were mobilized to fight in the Chickasaw War of the 1730s, the Choctaw War of the 1740s, and the English invasion scare of the 1750s. The policy led in turn to increased animosity between blacks and Indians, just as the French had intended.

Military service remained a constant part of the early black experience in Louisiana. As early as 1739, 270 blacks, 50 of them free, were under arms in Louisiana, and by the time Spain took control of the colony in 1770, the Louisiana militia included over 300 free black citizen soldiers.

Another region of early French-sponsored black settlement was the area then known as Upper Louisiana, or more precisely, the Illinois Territory. By the middle of the eighteenth century over 600 blacks lived in the Illinois region, most of them working as slaves for some 300 Frenchmen who were pioneering the development of the area. A principal occupation for African slaves in the Louisiana territories therefore was crewing the riverboats that were rowed up the Mississippi with trade goods for the Indians, arms and ammunition, and fresh troops and settlers for the northern posts. Both the trip upriver and the return with loads of flour, trade pelts, and more passengers were extremely arduous and dangerous. The river with its strong and treacherous currents was more than challenging; lying in wait for the unwary was a ruinous assortment of shifting sandbars, fearsome whirlpools, deadly driftwood rams, and hostile Indians. It should not be surprising that most of the crewmen for these early voyages were African immigrants who had been trained in river navigation by their experiences on the Senegal and Gambia Rivers of Africa.

One of the blacks who headed north from New Orleans as an independent hunter and trapper in this era was a Haitian of mixed blood named Jean Baptiste Pointe Du Sable. A British report of 1779 described him as "a handsome Negro, well educated and settled at Eschikagou, but . . . much in the interest of the French."[4] Du Sable lived for 16 years as a trapper and trader in a log cabin near Lake Michigan at the mouth of the Chicago River. He established a family there with his Indian wife, and his settlement would grow to include a 22- by 40-foot main house and a bakehouse, dairy, poultry house, workshop, stable, barn, and mill. He was said to have been cultured and prosperous enough that his home contained 23 pieces of imported European art, probably making him at the time the largest art collector west of the Alleghenies. Although Du Sable eventually sold his interest in the trading post—after losing an election to the chiefdomship of a neighboring Indian tribe in 1800—his settlement at Chicago would become one of the largest cities in the United States.

Looking to the south and west of the original 13 colonies into the Spanish and French territories that would also eventually become part of the United States reveals a large, active, and important African American presence in the colonial era. Understanding this history reinforces the idea that African American culture has always been far broader than Anglo-American culture, more comprehensively American, and American at an earlier date.

Part Three

Black Life in the English North American Colonies

eight

Moving toward Racial Slavery

> Moreover, of the children of the strangers that do sojourn among you, of them shall ye buy, and of their families that are with you, which they begat in your land; and they shall be your possession. And ye shall take them as an inheritance for your children after you, to inherit them for a possession; they shall be your bondsmen for ever.
>
> Leviticus 25: 45–46

> Blacks [are] the most useful appurtenances of a Plantation and perpetual servants.
>
> English Council for Foreign Plantations (1664)

For those Africans who arrived in English North America directly, the landing must have seemed a blessing after the horrors of the Middle Passage. The rolling of the sea finally stopped, and when the hatches were thrown back, in an explosion of blinding light, the inrush of sweet fresh air carried a promise of new beginnings. But as the new arrivals were herded down the gangplanks, they were still enslaved, still facing an unknown future. What kind of life awaited them in the new country? The answer was not so obvious as we might think.

African American slavery was not part of a preplanned development scheme for the English colonies. The British lacked sufficient experience with institutionalized slavery, racial caste, and Africa itself to have planned their strategy out beforehand. But a Western-European predisposition to use unfree labor was already there. Native Americans had quickly become targets for English enslavement because, as pagans holding desirable land, they were particularly vulnerable to the wars of colonial expansion; moreover, they knew the country and how to exploit it. But practical realities also made native laborers a shaky base upon which to build colonial prosperity: Indian servants could escape too easily into the surrounding wilderness, and many were fatally vulnerable to European diseases. In the seventeenth century, therefore, the native peoples captured in North American wars were more valuable sold off as slaves to the West Indies than as a local labor force.

Another group that might have satisfied colonial labor requirements without recourse to developing a new institution of racial slavery was to be found in the British homelands. Seventeenth-century Britain and Ireland seemed overrun with homeless, crime-prone folk wandering the countryside or crowding pestilentially into squalid urban slums. This growing underclass, along with a motley assortment of religious and political dissenters, provided British officials with a reservoir of ideal candidates for transportation to the new colonies. On the face of it, two problems could be solved with one solution: by transporting such people to the colonies, the social and political problems of the homeland would be reduced, and the colonies would have workers for the plantations that supplied needed exports to the mother country.

Such a two-pronged white labor scheme would not in itself have created the castelike bondage that marked later American slave labor arrangements. Because of the implications for class politics at home, Englishmen could not hold their countrymen to lifetime terms of service, not even in the far-off colonies. They could, however, place British subjects into service for a period of years to pay off the costs of their transportation and fines.

Nonetheless, even the best-intentioned schemes to profitably rehabilitate the idle poor in the colonies foundered when indentured servants proved a generally unruly lot with unseemly high ambitions to become the equals of their erstwhile masters. Moreover, when these countrymen ran away from their bondage, it was hard to be certain they were not the free citizens they immediately claimed to be, much less apprehend them.

Such had been the history of forced labor in English colonies when the first Africans were off-loaded from a Dutch slaver in 1619 and sold to the English settlers of Jamestown, Virginia. The little evidence we have suggests that these earliest African workers in the Chesapeake region were not treated as slaves but experienced terms and conditions of service roughly similar to those of the white indentured servants already in the colony, whom local residents already had been working for terms of four to seven years while they paid off the costs of their transportation. These first African Americans appear to have quickly learned that the possibilities of America might belong to them as much as to their white counterparts. Thus, between 1664 and 1677 at least 13 of these black workers bought or earned their liberty and settled alongside their white colonial countrymen as small landholders on tracts they purchased from richer white landowners; sometimes these ex-slaves even prospered enough to purchase servants of their own. By 1668 nearly one-third of the blacks in Northampton County were free, and their improving economic and social conditions suggest that their white neighbors originally thought of them as potential countrymen.

But when frontier conditions began to solidify along stricter class lines and land became too expensive to be purchased by those recently released from terms of service, the primary avenue for the advancement of African laborers was effectively closed. The rising price of land hurt them more than their white countrymen: they had to depend upon their own achievements for political protection, whereas most white immigrants held the rights of Englishmen by birth. Thus, when access to property was greatly reduced and landholding became limited to fewer and fewer hands, blacks lost their best hope for establishing enough political power in the settlements. African American servants were thus unable to defend themselves from exploitation when their white countrymen began to consider alternative models of social organization based upon the nearby slave colonies of the West Indies.

Almost from the beginning, white property owners across British North America suspected that colonial success would require the development of export economies based on racial slavery. And to a great extent the economic actions of individual planters who purchased unfree black laborers from the West Indies and continued to keep them as slaves preceded organized political analysis of the issue of life-term bondage. The unexamined price for adopting a slave labor system without first developing a political rationalization was an insidious incompatibility between the new economic and social realities of colonial slavery and the basic political ideology of British North America.

The American caste system the colonies were building was far too rigid to comfortably support an evolving political and social system premised on widely based and self-interested free choice both in the market and at the polls. The North American body politic began to grow twisted and deformed. Intellectually liberal democracy was an inspiring dream, but the physical reality of the colonies was becoming ever more monstrous as the rigidity of caste strained against the expanding ideology of personal freedom. The point of pain was where African Americans would come to live.

Much of the colonial era witnessed an unsuccessful attempt to reconcile two developing, but opposing, ways of life within a single, coherent body of national thought. This struggle is reflected in the false syllogism that Thomas Jefferson developed at the end of the era: although all men were created with equal rights, blacks were racially different men; therefore, they had no political freedoms that white Americans needed to recognize.

Racial bondage was adopted piecemeal by individual white settlers in the North American colonies before the English had been able to come to ideological terms with either race or slavery. The result was that, out of their different experiences, each of the colonies developed its own distinct system of slavery and race relations.

The Africans who came to the colonies had experience with slavery as a legal institution; almost all of them had been enslaved for a period in the Old

World before being shipped abroad. Therefore, they did not at first perceive their enslavement in America as either particularly unusual or particularly demeaning. Modern scholars have often and correctly pointed out that African slavery was not chattel slavery; it was an older and far more humane institution. But experience with bondage meant that the newly arriving Africans tended to accept enslavement as a natural social relationship, even though they might resist cruel treatment, or even enslavement itself, for themselves personally.

As a result of evolving European and African cultural attitudes, a new system of labor exploitation based essentially on West Indian precedents grew up on mainland North America. The change from indentures to lifetime enslavement did not seem as revolutionary to the Africans as it actually was to the English. The larger the number of blacks within a colony, the more it moved toward the West Indian model of slavery. Life was certainly different for blacks in each colony, yet everywhere in North America the growing repressions of slavery and racism were becoming part of daily experience.

Precisely because social and economic life differed between the colonies, Jefferson's fraudulent syllogism would face a serious challenge in the North after the American Revolution, when many former colonials began to reject slavery as ill suited to the political ideals of the new democracy. Unfortunately, by that time the growing racism that supported the expropriations of slavery had metastasized throughout the whole of English North America. That cancer, once spread, would take much longer to eradicate.

nine

New England

You have had the best of me, and you and yours must have the worst. Where am I to go in sickness or old age? No, Master, your slave I am, and always will be, and I will belong to your children when you are gone; and by you and them I mean to be cared for.

Rev. Mose Parsons's Connecticut slave, when offered his freedom in old age

The truth is, despite our nation's self-image as the land of the free, slavery was found in all of our original 13 colonies. Most Americans are aware that for a time the South was slave territory, but in the beginning slavery flourished in the northern colonies as well. Even New England, stereotyped as the home of town-meeting democracy and puritanical Christianity, was deeply involved in the Atlantic slave trade from the beginning; throughout the seventeenth and eighteenth centuries the New England colonies became home to increasing numbers of enslaved Africans and American-born blacks.

Like the rest of the North America colonies, New England had not been planned as a slaving region, and certainly its northern climate would not have immediately suggested the idea. But almost from the first years New Englanders had taken to the sea, and their skill in carrying cargoes across the ocean soon brought them into profound and corrupting contact with Atlantic slavery. Thus, it is not surprising that within a decade of the founding of Boston in 1630, the city's merchants had begun trading in black slaves and, almost as an afterthought, carrying a few bondspeople home for domestic work in New England. Trading in both Native American and African slaves was at that time considered a profitable and legitimate business, and over the years, in one connection or another, racial bondage became vital to the success of the Yankee economy.

Indeed, as early as 1645 Emanuel Downing, brother-in-law to Gov. John Winthrop of Massachusetts, was pining for a "just war" so that he could legally seize some Indians, whom he could later exchange for Negro slaves from the West Indies. The colony would never thrive, Downing explained to Winthrop, "until we get . . . a stock of slaves sufficient to do all our business," contending that 20 black slaves could be maintained for the cost of one white servant.[1] Although Downing was prone to exaggeration, others must have shared his views, because by 1715 there were over 12,000 African Americans living in the northern colonies, and most were in bondage. In fact, at the beginning of the eighteenth century one of every five slaves working in English North America was owned by a northern master, and the black population in the North was growing at the same pace as in the southern plantation colonies.[2]

The slave trade became even more important to New England during the years 1713–50, when English shippers, including colonials, won a monopoly to carry African slaves to the Spanish colonies. Rhode Island merchants, for example, averaged some 18 voyages a year to Africa in the three decades from 1730 to 1760. In fact, during the early eighteenth century New England became the preeminent slave-transporting region of the English colonies, although in the Atlantic slave trade as a whole Yankee traders played only a relatively small part. Moreover, most of the slaves carried in Yankee vessels went to and from the West Indies and southern mainland colonies rather than directly from Africa to New England.

New England ships were even more important to the slave systems of the West Indies and the mainland colonies as carriers of goods than of slave labor. For without ships to handle the oceanic transport of exports and imports, no slave-based colonial economy could have prospered. Yankee vessels carried vital cargoes of lumber, beans, grains, dairy products, and fish to the islands and mainland colonies where slaves were too valuable in producing exports to be able to fully meet their own subsistence needs.

In exchange for such necessities, Yankee captains carried away cargoes of slave-produced staples bound for Europe, often by way of New England. Moreover, using their own exports—such as light cloth, iron goods, and Yankee-made rum (which they distilled from West Indian molasses)—New Englanders set up a triangular trade carrying imported goods to Africa, slaves to the West Indies, and staples back home.

Direct African immigration to the New England region was always relatively small-scale; in the colonial period blacks never amounted to more than 3 percent of the Yankee population, the vast preponderance of which was English (see table 9.1). Nevertheless, New England was certainly a slaveholding region, and black laborers—many of them so-called refuse slaves from the West Indies—were imported in increasing numbers from the early 1600s to the time of the American Revolution.

TABLE 9.1
Estimated Black Colonial Population in 1750

Colony	Blacks	Total	Percentage Black
Founding Colonies:			
New Hampshire	600	27,600	2%
Massachusetts	4,100	188,000	2
Rhode Island	3,300	33,200	10
Connecticut	3,000	111,300	3
New York	11,000	76,700	14
New Jersey	5,400	71,400	8
Pennsylvania	2,900	119,700	2
Delaware	1,500	28,700	5
Maryland	43,500	141,100	31
Virginia	101,500	231,100	44
North Carolina	19,800	73,000	27
South Carolina	39,000	64,000	61
Georgia	1,000	5,200	19
Subtotal	236,600	1,171,000	20
Other Territories:			
East Texas	230	1,200	19
Florida	300	2,600	12
Louisiana	4,700	7,900	60
Total	241,830	1,182,700	20

Based on data in Jim Potter, "Demographic Development and Family Structure," in *Colonial British America: Essays in the New History of the Early Modern Era*, ed. Jack P. Greene and J. R. Pole (Baltimore, 1985), 137.

Because most northern slaves came into North America by way of the West Indies, it is impossible to determine with precision how many were born in Africa (or where in Africa) and how many were born in the West Indies. Nevertheless, most of the immigrants seem to have been African by birth and to have come originally from Senegambia and the Windward Coast, the Gold Coast, the Bight of Biafra, and Central Africa.

Conditions began to deteriorate for the New England slave economy by the middle of the eighteenth century. Because the staple exports produced by the middle and southern colonies with slave labor had become more and more valuable, markets for these products increased rapidly in Europe and slave prices rose. New England lacked such a regional specialty, however, and black slavery there became comparatively less profitable and therefore less important.

Large-scale slavery was unusual in the New England colonies because the indigenous New England economy, unlike the more tropical regions, simply did not need slaves to prosper. The cold climate, rocky soil, and long Yankee winters precluded the development of West Indian–style plantations using intensive slave labor to produce rich export crops. Only in the Narragansett section of Rhode Island and nearby Connecticut, where stock-raising, dairy-ing, and specialized tobacco growing proved possible, were large numbers of slaves put to work in something even approaching plantation-style labor. Although the short growing season and the poor-quality soil limited agricul-tural exports, most New Englanders were involved at least part-time in sub-sistence farming for local consumption. Therefore the majority of the region's African Americans, like their white countrymen, spent some of their hours in the fields.

Most Yankee masters owned only one or two servants who lived and worked alongside them as secondary members of a single household. Thus, the region's slaves not only labored beside whites, they usually lived with them as well. Slaves ate in the same kitchens as their masters—commonly at the same table—used the same privies, warmed themselves by the same fires, and slept in whatever vacant space was available, usually in an attic or out-building. Slave huts like those common in the plantation regions were rare in New England. When their service was needed, slaves were sometimes even required to sleep in the same rooms with their masters or mistresses, bedding down on the floor and sharing in whatever snoring disturbed the Yankee night.

Despite the region's reputation for fostering education, New England slaves were able to obtain little in the way of formal schooling. A few mission schools for Indians and blacks were established by groups like the Society for the Propagation of the Gospel in Foreign Parts, but they had no effect on the vast majority of the region's slaves. Informal education within the master's household was more common, and although a few Yankee masters forbade instruction in reading for slaves as disruptive to good discipline, many others made sure that their servants could read the Bible and work simple arithmetic.

The economics of a colder climate required most northern bondspeople to obtain skills beyond domestic service to pay for their upkeep during the long periods of the year when work in the fields was impossible. Although daily housework was expected of nearly all Yankee slaves, versatility in other areas was usually required as well. New England bondspeople worked alongside their masters as bakers, barbers, blacksmiths, and bookbinders; brick-makers, butchers, carpenters, chair-makers, chandlers, and chimney sweeps; cooks, coopers, distillers, dye-makers, ironworkers, and joiners; masons, miners, nail-ers, porters, pressmen, rope- and sail-makers; sawyers, shipwrights, shoemakers, stave-makers, spinners, tailors, tanners, teamsters, tinkers, and typesetters; watchmakers, weavers, whitesmiths, and woodsmen; and many other occupations. Outside the household, black women often labored independently as domestic helpers, washerwomen, and seamstresses.

The largest number of black laborers in New England resided in the maritime cities of the coast from Boston on down to Norwalk, Connecticut, where they were connected in one way or another with the region's nautical industries—shipping, slave-trading, whaling, fishing, naval construction, and the many service and support industries that undergirded the maritime way of life.

Slaves who lived in white New England families began to think of themselves as having a special relationship with their owners and their owners' household. Probably not coincidentally, the connection was perceived by slaves as almost a fictional kinship, like the long-term master-slave relationships in Africa. This black understanding of the familial relationship also fit well with Protestant religious theory, which held that the servants living under a master's roof were essentially in a filial relationship with the master and under his paternal guidance. Thus, when the question of baptism of African-born slave children came up, it was decided in New England that such black children could be baptized on the presumption of their master's salvation (rather than rejected on the basis of their natural parents' paganism) in exactly the same way that the master's own children were accepted into what was called the Half-way Covenant. Theologically speaking, in New England the salvation of master and slave were inextricably bound.

Given the physical and social closeness in which New England blacks and whites lived, vicious and cruel behavior toward slaves was far easier to control and discourage than it was where the social distance between masters and workers was much greater, or where whites were isolated from the social intervention of more compassionate peers. Nonetheless, bondage was still bondage.

New England, like other slaveholding regions, had to develop a system of legal controls not only to enforce enslavement upon its victims but to limit the cruelty of those who profited from its use. When the first slaves arrived, the English settlers had no precedents for organizing a society based on chattel slavery. Legally, black servants, like their white counterparts, were originally expected to be freed after a term of service, but for blacks, that English precedent was generally disregarded. Instead, because most of the early slaves were imported from the West Indies, Yankee masters found it easy to adopt the alternative West Indian model of lifetime terms of enslavement, which offered the greatest possibility to exploit unprotected black laborers.

New England masters soon passed into legislation a growing body of severe laws designed to put a damper on slave resistance to bondage. Curfews made it illegal for slaves to move about after dark, and violators who dared to go out to see friends or loved ones were liable to undergo public whipping if caught. Even nominally legal social gatherings of blacks, mulattoes, and Indians greatly annoyed and sometimes frightened New England townsmen, and new laws were constantly passed to discourage them. By the middle of the eighteenth century, when more blacks began arriving directly from Africa, Massachusetts, like the southern colonies, moved to ban the royal "parades," "pageants and other shews" that were so important to black holiday celebrations in New England and across most of the New World.

Boston authorities succeeded in banning formal public displays of African American racial pride, but they were not able to suppress the holiday gatherings of blacks on election days, which even slaves claimed as their right. Elsewhere in the region, however, black bondspeople commonly won their masters' permission to celebrate "Negro 'Lection Day," with the formal election of black kings and governors who, once chosen, were honored with large inaugural parades and grand ceremonies symbolizing both the heritage of Africa and a growing African American sense of nationality. The black officers elected, although not part of the official white governmental structure, were permitted to rule indirectly over African American populations in cities like Newport, Hartford, and Portsmouth, where they typically judged minor criminal and civil complaints brought against African Americans by both whites and blacks.

The New England "Negro Election" celebrations, which reached their height during the late eighteenth century, were much like similar observances all over the Americas (except in the American South), and their significance as a nationalist statement is important. For although black New Englanders were the most assimilated group of African Americans in the English colonies, they had already adopted by the late eighteenth century a double consciousness of themselves as both African and American, a dual identity that W. E. B. Du Bois later said felt like having two warring souls in the same body.

ten

New York and the Middle Colonies

My grandfather's grandmother was seized by an evil Dutch
trader two centuries ago; and coming to the valleys of the
Hudson and Housatonic, black, little and lithe, she shivered and
shrank in the harsh north winds, looked longingly at the hills,
and often crooned a heathen melody to the child between her
knees, thus:

> Do ba-no co-ba, ge-ne me, ge-ne me!
> Do ba-na co-ba, ge-ne me, ge-ne me!
> Ben d' nu-li, nu-li, ben d'le!

The child sang it to his children and they to their children's children, and so 200 years it has traveled down to us and we sing it
to our children, knowing as little as our fathers what its words
may mean, but knowing well the meaning of its music.

W. E. B. Du Bois, "Africa and the American Negro
Intelligentsia" (1954)

In New York slavery was far more important than in New England. When
the Dutch held the territory between 1624 and 1664, they had been interested in carrying slaves to New Netherland both to develop the area and to
increase trade for their own shipping business with the African coast.
Although the profit-seeking Dutch used New Netherland as a destination for
their Atlantic slave trade from Angola, their colonial outpost was not yet a
large market for direct African imports.

The first slaves carried into the colony were employed by the Dutch West
India Company to build palisades and fortifications on Long Island—such as
the blockhouse at Oyster Bay—to protect the Dutch settlement from both

Native Americans and marauding English. In such battles the African new-comers were expected to take up arms and fight alongside the trading company's troops.

Masters in New Netherland preferred slaves who had been seasoned on the island of Curaçao rather than ones carried directly from Africa; seasoned bondspeople who knew some Dutch were far easier to work with than those imported directly. Even so, the earliest New York colonists could afford few slaves from any region, although they were convinced that slave labor would be necessary to the colony's ultimate success.

The Swedish colonists who began settling in western New Jersey along the Delaware Bay after 1638 were likewise persuaded from the New York experience that American colonization was impossible without African slave labor, and so they also quickly added Negroes to their labor force.

Although the blacks imported into New Netherland were far fewer in number than those taken to the Dutch slave colonies in the West Indies, they made a major impact locally. When the Dutch West India Company ship *Gideon* arrived in New York in 1664, it carried some 300 African slaves; such a number would not have been exceptional in the Caribbean, but in New Netherland the new Africans expanded the colony's population by 5 percent.

Later in the same year the Second Anglo-Dutch War resulted in the English taking control of the territories they would call New York, New Jersey, and Delaware. Under the British, slaving continued unabated. Like their Dutch predecessors, the English in New York imported more than twice as many new slaves by way of the West Indies as directly from Africa. Until 1750 most of those arriving straight from the continent were children under 13, who were preferred by local buyers because they could be trained for work in their master's intimate household.

Throughout the colonial period imports of slaves from the West Indies and Africa remained extremely important to New York's success, so much so that between 1732 and 1754 well over one-third of the immigrants arriving through the port of New York were black bondspeople. During the first half of the eighteenth century the black population of New York grew rapidly, from around 2,300 people, or around 11 percent of the colony's total population, to over 11,000, or 15 percent of the total (see table 9.1). In the 1750s and 1760s the importation of adult Africans increased, but it rapidly declined after 1770, when the price of slaves became too high for the local market. As importation fell off, the black percentage of the colony's population began to decline, falling back to around one in ten at the time of the American Revolution.

Within the colony slaving was most important on Long Island and along the lower Hudson River Valley, where sizable, plantationlike estates supported relatively intense and large-scale slave-labor farming on a par with the plantations of the southern colonies. Indeed, around half of the eighteenth-century workforce in the lower Hudson Valley was of African heritage, making that area far more like Tidewater Virginia than like nearby New England.

Overall, New Yorkers held many more slaves than anyone else in the northern colonies; in fact, the 15 percent of New York's total population in 1750 who were slaves compared to a black population in New England of only about 3 percent at the same time. Moreover, by the late colonial period, proportionally more households contained slaves in the hinterland of New York City than in the whole of any southern state; during most of the eighteenth century New York City trailed only Charleston, South Carolina, in the size of its black population.

New slaves arriving in New York were often sold at dockside, but slave auctions were also held at least weekly at the Merchant's Coffee House, the Fly Market, or the Proctor's Vendue House. In 1790, as the colonial period ended, about 40 percent of the white households around New York City owned slaves, and blacks made up nearly one-quarter of the urban population.

The size of the slaveholding units in the city was usually quite small; typically, as in New England, one or two slaves lived in the same residence as their master. In both regions urban slaves were encouraged to develop great labor versatility. In the New York colony as a whole, however, farmers were twice as likely as townspeople to own slaves. Rural slaves worked primarily in agriculture, but they also provided the skilled craft labor necessary to fill out the regional economy. The work of rural slaves was usually arranged around a task system: the bondspeople managed their own time and rate of work as long as they finished the tasks at hand.

In urban areas across the North masters commonly had no interest in raising large slave families and were liable to sell slave women in their childbearing years because they could not afford more servants. In areas where slaves lived with their masters, the inconvenience and expense of small children were often deciding factors in slave sales. Sometimes, however, this factor worked the other way: a master would purchase a slave infant to help his wife cope with the loss of a baby.

Much as in New England, small-scale slave-owning in New York often took the form of a family system of slavery, with whites and blacks working and living side by side, although in different class positions. And also as in New England, such intensely personal contact encouraged a milder form of slavery than was typical of plantation slavery farther to the south. But better physical treatment based on the closeness of the races carried its own price for the African American community: black slaves living in white households were often separated from their own families and communities.

In cities such as New York and Philadelphia, where African American laborers were often required to work a variety of jobs, many urban slaves possessed skills equal to or better than those of the best white artisans. Moreover, black apprentices were easier for masters to control, and black tradespeople were less expensive. As a result, black labor became increasingly important across the northern colonies. The frustration of skilled white workers competing unsuccessfully for jobs was at first directed more against slavery than the slaves, but after bondage was ended in the North, black workers became the target. Clearly, and ironically, some of the seeds of future racial conflict were laid in the growing fears of white workers that they could not compete successfully without some form of racial preference in hiring and wage rates.

Following a pattern similar to New York's, New Jersey and Delaware also became slave colonies, beginning with the Dutch communities along the Hudson River and the Swedish and Dutch settlements along the Delaware. Slavery expanded quickly once the English took control; in 1664 the proprietors of New Jersey, for example, began offering 45 acres of land for each new slave imported. In 1678 the town authorities in New Castle, Delaware, requested permission to trade with nearby Maryland for black servants. They had come to the conclusion shared by so many other North American colonials—that they could not survive, much less prosper, without the support of Negro slave labor.

As was the case elsewhere, the slaves imported into New Jersey were not evenly spread throughout the colony. By 1745 almost three-quarters of New Jersey bondspeople were concentrated in the eastern counties near New York; slaves were especially common in Perth Amboy, where almost all the white inhabitants owned at least one bondsperson. New Jersey's dependence on slave labor was somewhere between that of New York and New England: in the middle of the eighteenth century about 5,400 people, or 8 percent of the colony's population, were slaves, with far more of them residing in the Dutch eastern part of the colony than in the Quaker west (see table 9.1).

Despite Pennsylvania's Quaker origins, settlers there never questioned the need for African slaves during the colony's formative years. When a shipload of Africans were offered for sale in Philadelphia in 1684, the earliest Quaker settlers snapped them up so eagerly that almost no specie remained in town with which to buy anything else. William Penn would later explain that he preferred slaves over indentured white servants because an investment in slaves lasted the lifetime of the worker.

These first purchases were probably motivated by the strenuous work that faced new settlers in clearing the land and erecting the first crude houses. Pacifist and religious though they might have been, Quaker masters apparently drove their new slaves hard: only a few weeks after the arrival of a slave ship in Philadelphia, one of the new slave owners complained that his two best Africans had run off before he could profit from them at all.

As in New England, Philadelphia merchants often ordered small numbers of slaves from Barbados or elsewhere in the West Indies to be included in their more general cargoes. As the years passed, the colony's slaves tended to be concentrated in the commercial counties around Philadelphia, and by 1693 enough slaves had arrived in the Philadelphia area that authorities were complaining about what they called "the tumultuous gatherings of the Negroes in the town."[1]

In the late 1750s Philadelphia merchants began importing greater numbers of slaves directly from Africa; the largest shipment of them, some 500 mostly from Gambia, arrived in 1762. The city soon had a population nearly 8 percent black. On the wharves and in the supporting shops of the city between 15 and 20 percent of the workers were African American, and black women worked as cooks and domestics for most of the city's richer households.

Despite Philadelphia's large Quaker presence, the city made little concerted effort to educate its African American population. The Bray Associates opened a school for Negroes in 1750, and Anthony Benezet offered evening tutoring for both free and slave blacks in his home, based on the lessons he offered white pupils during the day. But neither effort reached more than a tiny fraction of those blacks who were eager to learn.

In colonial Pennsylvania as a whole, slave owners were in a small minority, and few of those who did own servants had more than four; usually there were no more than one or two slaves per slaveholding family. Urban gatherings on Sundays, holidays, and fair days were therefore the only way African Americans could enjoy communal social activities.

Although the numbers varied greatly from area to area in the colony, only somewhere around 3,000 slaves lived and worked in Pennsylvania by the middle of the eighteenth century—a number that constituted only around 2 percent of the colony's population (see table 9.1), a significant decline from the proportion of nearly 10 percent of the population in 1730. The importation of new slaves, whether from Africa or by way of the West Indies, came to a virtual standstill in the middle colonies after 1766 and effectively ended with the American Revolution.

eleven

The Chesapeake

They import so many Negroes hither, that I fear this Colony will some time or other be confirmed by the Name of New Guinea.

William Byrd II of Virginia to the Earl of Egmont (1736)

The number of Negroes in the southern colonies is upon the whole nearly equal, if not superior, to that of the white men; and they propagate and increase even faster.

Andrew Burnaby, *Travels through the Middle Settlements in North America* (1760)

In the lands along Chesapeake Bay, a temperate climate and fertile soil promised good yields to settlers who found the right crops and were willing to provide sufficient labor. The first ventures such as Jamestown failed because many of the gentlemen adventurers were both unwilling to work and ignorant of what to grow and how to grow it. Soon men more accustomed to hard labor were enticed to the colonies by promises of receiving land after several years of service; their arrival helped, although the death rates for such immigrants remained extremely high, owing to the difficult ocean crossing and the primitive conditions of the new settlements.

Moreover, the original native inhabitants were resisting the expansion of European settlements with military counterattacks, which took many additional lives. No wonder then that the idea of copying the Spanish precedent of importing African slaves to take up the slack soon gained some attention. But it was a sluggish process, as we have seen in the previous chapters. Planters preferred to work with their countrymen rather than with foreigners, and so over the decades of the seventeenth century the slave trade grew slowly, expanding impressively only after the supply of British labor began to dry up.

The slave trade became important in the Chesapeake region late in the seventeenth century when tobacco, with its large labor requirements, was established as a profitable staple export. Even so, by 1680 there were only about 4,000 slaves in the lands around Chesapeake Bay. By the late 1690s, however, the importation of Africans had rapidly expanded the black population. Especially numerous were men and women from the Niger Delta region; more than one-third of the newcomers originated from the Bight of Biafra. Others came from Senegambia, the Gold Coast, and Angola; in fact, about one-half of the upper South's slave immigrants came from these three regions.

Still, as the seventeenth century ended, the vast majority of Chesapeake planters held only a slave or two to work beside them in the fields; no more than a few of the largest planters held significantly larger numbers. Yet slavery was clearly becoming essential to the regional economy, and by the middle of the eighteenth century whatever skilled labor a local planter needed—milling, masonry, carpentry, smithing, cooperage, tanning, and the like—was likely to be supplied by African American workers. Black women specialized as soap-makers, starch-makers, and dyers in addition to the usual female chores.

Initially the introduction of Africans caused no major changes in the Chesapeake system of production begun during the seventeenth century; plantation operations had already developed a slaverylike routine for white workers featuring separate quarters for unfree servants, group labor under overseers, correction by whipping, and chronically insufficient food and clothing for members of the serving class. By the middle of the eighteenth century the biggest difference resulting from the use of African labor was that, though they cost more at purchase, black slaves could be held to lifetime tenures of service. Since new slaves so often died during their first few years in the Chesapeake, it was still a major gamble to make a lifetime investment in a slave with so little assurance that he or she would survive more than a year or so.

The death rates of new slaves declined as the seventeenth century progressed; with the increasing value of tobacco exports, Chesapeake planters replaced their diminishing supply of immigrant white workers with African slaves. One political consequence was a reduction in political divisions within white society as the white working class became smaller, and thereby less dangerous and frightening.

Most white laborers in Virginia came to support the growing caste system of racial supremacy, apparently because it was a system from which all whites could profit, at least in theory. Certainly the developing racial caste system made democracy among the white male citizenry less ominous than it had been under the older colonial system, when a class of poor but well-armed and edgy white frontiersmen (and their black allies) occasionally rose in insurrections, such as Bacon's Rebellion of 1676.

With the institutionalization of racial slavery, an unstable class of armed and angry white indentured servants holding the rights of Englishmen was replaced by a generally unarmed, black slave-labor caste placed clearly outside the political system. Ironically, the theoretical political equality of white colonials that slavery reinforced was increasing precisely as practical economic equality among Chesapeake whites was decreasing, for the heavy capital expenses of slave-based monoculture were seriously reducing entry into the planter class. Placing black Africans into a slave caste was one way to resolve growing class antagonism among whites.

Support for developing a new American political system depended upon building a racial unity among white males that would make the growing social and economic inequalities among them seem less compelling. This unity was built in part by an ever-tightening series of legal codes, such as those passed in Virginia in 1667, 1672, 1680, 1682, and 1688 designed to shove blacks ever farther down a spiral of dishonor, with right after right stripped away. The diminishment of black status was continued in the early years of the eighteenth century with bans on intermarriage, black testimony in court, and black voting. As black status fell away, poor whites seemed to rise in comparison—a perception that cost the colonial elite nothing.

In the frontier conditions of the seventeenth century most Virginia slaves had lived in their masters' primitive dwellings, shared toilet facilities with whites, and slept in nearby kitchens or outbuildings; when a more castelike and class-based system developed in the richer eighteenth century, housing on the larger plantations became separated by race, with slaves, except for a few house servants, moving together into small clusters of slave huts called quarters, usually located at some distance from the larger residence of the white master's family. Married couples often had their own small dwellings in the quarters, but single slaves lived together, four to six adults in a hut, with very little space for socializing within the small cabins.

The latter hardship may have been mitigated by the fact that there was so little free time a black man could call his own, and even less for a black woman. Even in the Chesapeake, the colonial era expected great versatility from slave laborers; if a worker was not in the field or on the waterways, something else could always be found that needed doing. Consider what the following two eighteenth-century Virginia advertisements imply about the work routines of Chesapeake slaves. A runaway named Deadfoot was described as "an indifferent shoemaker, a good butcher, ploughman, and carter; an excellent sawyer, and waterman, and understands breaking oxen well, and is one of the best scythemen . . . ; so ingenious a Fellow, that he can turn his hand to any thing"; another notice offered for sale "a Likely young Negro wench, about 25 years of age, she has a child of two months old, understands cooking, making paste, pickling, washing, ironing, cleaning house, and spinning."[1]

In good weather, slaves on the small farms and plantations of Virginia, Maryland, and northeastern North Carolina were expected to work at one job or another from dawn to dusk, taking only a couple of breaks for meals. Sundays and Christmas could be used for recreation, but slaves having too good a time tended to disturb their masters' sense of propriety. After tasks were finished on Sundays, slaves could devote time to the small garden plots in which they grew food of their own. Fishing was a another leisure pastime that provided some of the best meals available to a slave, and fish dishes were all the more enjoyable because they owed nothing to the master.

Sometimes the area's bondspeople were put to work in more industrial pursuits. In 1732 the Virginian William Byrd learned that 120 slaves, both men and women, were working at the Chiswell iron mines and works below Fredericksburg, and in the region's small cities white tradesmen often apprenticed unfree black laborers who later hired out their own time in a kind of semibondage.

Conditions in the Chesapeake began changing significantly during the eighteenth century as more Africans entered the region. Between 1700 and the American Revolution nearly 100,000 unfree African workers were imported into Virginia. The largest number were from the coastal societies around the Bight of Biafra and along the Gold Coast, but others arrived in significant numbers from the Angola region. Since these newcomers were picked on the basis of the labor that could be wrung out of them, twice as many men were imported as women. Thus, Thomas Cable, a merchant on Virginia's Eastern Shore, suggested in 1725 that if he "could choose a Cargoes of Negroes as you propose 200—I would have 100 men able young Slaves, 60 women, 30 Boys and 10 Girls from 10 to 14 years of age. Such a Cargoe could sell to great advantage."[2]

At first the natural increase of the black population was slow because there were so many men and so few women; moreover, those black women who lived in the Chesapeake region were worked hard, married late, and had few children. In 1740 around half of all slaves in Virginia were still African-born, but after midcentury the natural increase of the African American community grew rapidly, frightening many white observers like Virginia's Peter Fontaine, who warned his brothers that the slaves would soon "overrun a dutiful colony."[3] By 1790 the majority of the black population was both born in America and enslaved, so as the colonial era ended the need for additional foreign labor—white or black—was becoming incidental. Certainly in the years leading up to the American Revolution the Virginia colony was a very African American place, with blacks making up some 44 percent of the colony's total population (see table 9.1); in the tidewater region more than two of every three people were black.

Since revolutionary Virginia was the home of so many of our nation's "Founding Fathers" and first presidents, the predominance of blacks in the colony leads to some interesting speculation. Throughout the course of American history, the enslavement of blacks and notions of national freedom have been intimately connected. The willingness of the white colonial elite of

Virginia to allow the expansion of democracy in the first place was directly related to perhaps the central irony of American freedom. The white male citizens of Virginia were trusted with arms and political independence only after a totally nondemocratic system of racial slavery had been instituted. Apparently with enough land and labor to go around, white men expected that they would not have to exploit one another to survive and so could treat each other as equals.

But the political freedom enjoyed by white males was not itself based upon the abstract political principles so often cited as the source of American liberties. Instead, in the home of the Founding Fathers, democracy for the few was based on force and injustice: that is, on lands taken by conquest from the indigenous peoples, and on a system of unfree labor that featured political exclusion and a castelike slavery. The revolutionary leaders of Virginia were acutely concerned about issues of freedom and tyranny precisely because their own position lay somewhere between what they feared might be total subordination to the political elite of their mother country and what they hoped would be total domination over the laboring class of their own plantations.

Breaking English workers of their class attitudes and promoting ideas of race-based caste was not as easy as it might seem. Among the poor servants of the Chesapeake, white women sometimes took black lovers, and the resulting miscegenation was far different from that practiced by white males, who used power and status to gain sexual access to black women by either force or favor. Strict laws had to be both enacted and enforced to stop the continued crossing of caste lines by white females; white women violating the law found themselves given long terms of service, and the children of their unions were usually sold into near-slavery. The decision to treat the child of an interracial union as darker than his or her white parent, instead of lighter than the black parent, was economic rather than biological, for the net effect was to expand the base of exploitable labor while decreasing the size of the dominant caste.

Both whites and blacks had to learn how to deal with the unnatural restrictions of a caste society, but blacks paid by far the greater price. Consider the complaints of the Moravian Collegium of Salem, North Carolina, in 1776 about local interracial gatherings: "Our Brethren are too friendly with the Negroes and afterwards they are amazed at their freshness," and, "The main fault with our Brethren is that they are always with the Negroes in jokes and fun, and the next day they beat them like dogs."[4]

Because we know how history turned out, at least for our own time, we often think that what has happened must have been destined to occur. Thus, because our era has been one of racism and increasing economic and political inequality, we assume that the colonial era must have provided the unstable foundation of caste and class upon which our flawed modern political democracy was built. There is much evidence, however, that this was only partially the case in the seventeenth and early eighteenth centuries and that there was not a racial inevitability to our national history.

Slavery and capitalism were never harmonious partners, but during the colonial era the two institutions worked together in a kind of marriage of convenience. Capitalistic merchants willingly served as middlemen transporting unfree workers from Africa to plantations in America; moreover, capitalist enterprises were only too eager to profit on both sides of the Atlantic where precapitalist understandings of labor had not yet opened to the possibility that a market in wage labor could supply necessary work in an orderly, humane, and efficient way.

European merchants voraciously purchased the raw materials produced on American plantations, just as they actively worked to sell goods of both foreign and domestic manufacture to Africans. And on the ships that plied the Atlantic with cargoes of suffering slaves going one way and holds filled with addicting tobacco returning from the other, the crews worked for wages or for shares. Capitalism clearly profited off the human misery of slavery, but it did not directly cause it. Indeed, the northwestern Europeans who had taken the middleman's position were already learning the secret of modern productive labor: the voluntary decision by workers to offer their labor not out of obligation to their families or after being coerced by serfdom or bondage, but in return for wages—that is, out of self-interest.

Though the English continued to develop more productive systems of slavery from the seventeenth century through the nineteenth, forced labor never became all that efficient. In fact, from early in the seventeenth century many masters perceived that slaves, especially the highly skilled and better workers, were often more productive when used like wage laborers—switched from job to job as the need arose, and given the motivating opportunity to profit from their own work, perhaps sometimes even to buy their own freedom.

African Americans, both slave and free, were quick to fill the gaps in the colonial economy with their own entrepreneurial enterprise. Slaves commonly tried to merchandise small trade or food items, but in the Chesapeake world such selling was discouraged and had to be done at night. Black women across the Caribbean traded in a variety of products in large markets, but these were not permitted in Virginia, Maryland, or North Carolina, and most Chesapeake masters did not give their slaves sufficient provisioning grounds to produce a salable surplus of food, as was common in the West Indies. As a result, Chesapeake slave owners generally considered any items carried off their plantations by their black workers to be stolen. That the exchanges usually took place in the countryside at night with buyers from the poorer white class doubtless did not make such trading appear any more legitimate.

Elsewhere in the Americas, chickens, eggs, fish, and fresh vegetables were sometimes marketed openly by slaves, but in the Chesapeake such items were traditionally bartered only with the master, who most often gave in exchange goods such as lard, meat, and linen. The result of this discouragement of markets and marketing in the Chesapeake was an unfortunate withering away of the entrepreneurial tradition among most of the region's African Americans.

By monopolizing both economic resources and outlets, white Americans in the English North American colonies discouraged black economic enterprise in the same way that many non-Western societies are said to have discouraged the development of capitalist institutions. This outcome was not attributable to slavery itself, for in the West Indies slavery was able to coexist with a limited range of black entrepreneurial ventures. Instead, it appears to have been an early variant of rigging the economic system so as to limit competition and ensure higher profits than would result from a truly functional free market. In regard to colonial white and black relations, even the markets were not free.

twelve

The Lower South

Carolina looks more like a negro country than like a country settled by white people.

Samuel Dyssli, on visiting South Carolina (1737)

Our Staple Commodity for some years has been Rice and Tilling,
Planting, Hoeing, Reaping, Threshing, Pounding have all been
done merely by the poor Slaves here. Labour and the Loss of
many of their Lives testified the Fatigue they Underwent, in
Satiating the Inexpressible Avarice of their Masters.

Alexander Garden, report on South Carolina to the Royal
Society of Arts (1755)

It's shocking to human Nature, that any Race of Mankind and
their Posterity, should be sentenced to perpetual Slavery; nor in
Justice can we think otherwise of it, than they are thrown
among us to be our Scourge one Day or another, for our Sins;
and as Freedom to them must be as dear [as] to us, What a Scene
of Horror it must bring about!

Inhabitants of New Inverness, Georgia, petition against slavery
(1739)

A Man at the end of 8 years, who plants with white men is
£715.99 worse, than he would be were he to use Negroes: and
Such at present is the difference in planting on the North and
South sides of the River Savannah.

Thomas Stephens, *Observations on the Present State of Georgia*
(1740)

Not counting those Negroes who blended in with the local Indians during the
Spanish expeditions of the sixteenth century, the earliest black settlers of the

73

English Carolinas arrived as slaves in present-day South Carolina in 1670 with the first fleet of English colonizers. Since many of the whites in this original party were from Barbados, they carried with them the vision of a wealthy slave colony based upon the West Indian model. Also part of this group was the first black family in Carolina. We know little about them except that they were slaves and part of the household of the new governor, William Sayle. Their names were recorded as "John Sr., Elizabeth, and John Jr."

In the succeeding years more Africans were imported into South Carolina from the Gold Coast, Senegambia, the Windward Coast, and Angola than from anywhere else in Africa. Local masters preferred slaves from the rice-growing regions of the Windward Coast and Senegambia, but their high price often dictated the substitution of slaves from Central Africa. Indeed, during the eighteenth century the largest representation of slaves brought into the colony, nearly 40 percent, were from the Congo-Angola region; the ethnic makeup of South Carolina slaves was therefore quite different from the prevailing makeup in colonies farther to the north, where slaves from the Niger Delta region were more common. Since most of the slaves entering Georgia and North Carolina came first through the port of Charleston, the ethnic makeup of those two colonies was generally similar to South Carolina's.

To encourage the importation of much needed labor, each Carolina planter was given the rights to 20 acres of land for each black male imported into the colony as a slave and 10 acres for each woman imported. During the earliest years as many as one-third of the new arrivals were Negroes, and as the land rewards would suggest, most were men. It was hoped by English officials that black and white settlers together would prove a barrier to Spanish expansion from out of Florida. For the South Carolina elite, however, Africans were the laborers of choice because of their invaluable economic skills, especially their superior knowledge of rice and indigo cultivation and free-range animal husbandry.

One of the first jobs given to African slaves was the tending of free-range cattle. It was not coincidental that South Carolina imported many West Africans from the Senegambia region, where experienced cattle-keepers were common. Such West Africans doubtless influenced the South Carolina techniques of open grazing (with nightly penning for protection) and seasonal burning of the open lands to freshen the grasses. The historian Peter H. Wood has speculated that the term *cowboy* may in fact have been first used in pejorative reference to these African American cattle herders.[1]

Even more important to the success of South Carolina was the knowledge of wet-rice agriculture that Africans brought with them from the Windward Coast and Madagascar. Thus, American rice-growing techniques, as the historian Daniel C. Littlefield has shown, came to mirror those used in Africa: Carolina swamps were cleared, slash-and-burn style, in preparation for planting; hollowed-out tree trunks were used to drain the soil; and dikes were constructed to control seasonal flooding.[2] On both sides of the ocean black workers used long-handled, flat-tongued shovels to turn the soil and short-handled hoes to work it. Rice farming was extremely arduous, for much of the weeding had to be done by slaves working in hot and humid conditions in stooped-over positions, knee-deep in stagnant water. The work gangs tried to ease the burden and monotony of their tasks by improvisational call-and-response singing—working in unison to the traditional communal rhythms that undergirded an ever-changing subject matter. When the rice crop was harvested, the grains were winnowed with the same kind of wide, flat baskets that were used in Africa and then husked in African-style wooden mortars with pestles wielded by black women pounding out rhythmic patterns that would have been familiar enough to their mothers on the old continent.

Many of the imported Africans spoke more than one African language, and some had served as professional linguists. Others held positions in the colonies similar to that of Timboe, a black man who nominally watched the packhorses but far more importantly negotiated with the Creeks as agent for a Savannah trader. So successful was Timboe as an interpreter that in 1717 his "extraordinary service" was rewarded with a £60 extra commission; most of this extra compensation, however, was taken by his master rather than going to the talented slave.

During the entire colonial period the hardest labor in building a successful economy was assigned to black slaves. It was they who created South Carolina's basic infrastructure—cutting forests, building roads, opening canals, draining swamps, preparing ricelands—and it was also the blacks who hauled and loaded commodities, cleaned up Charleston's refuse, and fished from and rowed the smaller boats up and down local rivers. In these jobs they faced more than their share of the deadly fevers that seemed to rise out of the Carolina swamps during fever season. It is primarily their accomplishments to which the success of South Carolina should be credited.

The area of African American expertise that offered some of the greatest autonomy for its practitioners was fishing. Black fishermen dominated the Carolina fishing industry and were permitted to own their own boats, canoes, and nets. In fishing families the men fished and the women—following the earlier West African pattern—marketed the catch as street vendors or from small fish stalls.

During the seventeenth century in Carolina, most black laborers worked alongside whites in relative harmony, for both groups were living together, armpit to armpit, in a crude and necessarily intimate frontier existence. By the early eighteenth century a few larger plantations had been built, and class differentiation quickly increased. More and more, the colony's richer whites became absentee landlords during the hotter part of the year, when the yearly fevers were most prevalent and deadly. The result along the Carolina coast was that slaves, working under a task system that fostered independence and self-discipline, enjoyed an increasing racial separation and a great deal of interaction among themselves. As Rev. Alexander Garden, a missionary for the

Society for the Propagation of the Gospel in Foreign Parts, wrote in a letter to the Society, the region's blacks were "a Nation within a Nation. In all country settlements, they live in Contiguous houses, and often 2, 3 or 4 families of them in one House. . . . They labour together and converse almost wholly among themselves."[3]

Unfortunately, precisely because the colony was becoming blacker and more dependent on slave labor, the master class worried about the potential for slave revolts like those that racked neighboring Jamaica. Thus, the increasing separation of the races in Carolina was paralleled by an increasing racial repression. To attract more white workers so as to better balance the population, more and more of the skilled jobs that blacks had begun to dominate at the beginning of the century were increasingly reserved for whites. Black frustration quickly increased and led in 1739 to the major, but unsuccessful, Stono uprising, which we shall examine later.

When the Stono revolt demonstrated the downside of depending so much on slave labor, Carolina's white authorities tried to solve the problem by making local bondage more tolerable and yet more restrictive. A prohibitive duty was placed on the importation of new slaves so as to diminish the danger of continuing to import dangerous revolutionaries like the Angolans who organized the Stono revolt; fewer slave imports would also reduce the threatening growth rate of the black population. At the same time colonial officials passed the Negro Act, which reduced black freedoms significantly; the negative effect on the black population of Carolina was only slightly offset by new laws under which masters could be penalized for overly brutal treatment of their slaves.

When Georgia was founded in 1733, a conscious decision was made to prohibit black slavery in the territory. The trustees of the colony hoped to achieve three goals by settling poor but hardworking white families along the southern borderland: they would relieve poverty in Britain while reforming the idle poor; they would build a buffer zone against Spanish expansion; and they would increase the wealth of the empire. Slave labor would clearly defeat at least two of these purposes. Slavery would corrupt the morals of the worthy poor by creating a culture of white idleness and luxury; moreover, settling slaves on the frontier would undermine colonial defenses by creating a potential fifth column to be exploited by both the Spanish and local Indians.

For the next 15 years Georgia struggled with its worthy resolve to do without bondage before eventually succumbing to the economic desires of inhabitants who saw themselves falling behind their slaveholding neighbors. To explain the situation to Parliament, Thomas Stephens in 1740 wrote a paper entitled *Observations on the Present State of Georgia* in which he argued that at the end of eight years a Georgia planter with white laborers would be more than £700 worse off than if he had used Negroes. Although Stephens exaggerated, it has been estimated that in the 1740s it cost about nine pounds in clothes and food to keep a white male servant, as opposed to only three and a half pounds for a black slave, who was not expected to dress or eat as well. The failure of Georgia's original intentions to redeem the white poor through their own hard work clearly illustrates a general belief among Americans of the colonial era that whites could not successfully colonize North America without the contributions of African labor.

Between 1751, when slavery was first legally sanctioned in Georgia, and 1775, the colony's black population grew from around 1,000 to close to 15,000 souls (or nearly half the population), most of whom were African by birth. Of the slaves born outside the colony, over half were imported directly from Africa, with Gambia (loosely defined) the favorite source; another one-third or more came by way of the West Indies.

Ironically, once slavery was permitted, Georgia almost entirely departed from the founders' original intention to uplift the character of the downtrodden. Georgia masters had no intention of seeing Negro bondspeople aspire to anything higher than servitude. In fact, by law they tried to make sure that blacks would not be permitted to develop any habits of self-improvement. Thus, although Africans were very interested in literacy, the colony's slave codes forbade masters to teach their slaves to read and write.

Training in crafts such as barrel-making and carpentry were sometimes permitted because such labor was badly needed, but slaves were discouraged from using their skills to their own advantage, such as by charging market rates when they hired themselves out. Instead, commissioners in Savannah received permission to set artificially low rates for compensating slave artisans. Moreover, Georgia authorities banned blacks from keeping cattle on their own; although this prohibition was probably intended to prevent rustling, it served as yet another impediment to black economic enterprise.

Thus, even in the margins of slavery that might have permitted enterprising individuals to aspire to economic improvement and self-motivation, African Americans found the way barred; free market capitalism may have been growing in the white labor market, but for Georgia blacks it was too often not a legal option. The colony had come full circle: from its original and revolutionary intention of redeeming the worthy poor by giving them the opportunity to better themselves, thereby increasing both social equality and the general wealth, Georgia had become a retrogressive caste society that held its poorest citizens back, consciously destroying their initiative so as to protect the wealth of the few.

When the British defeated the French in 1763, thus ending the Seven Years' War, Great Britain became the owner of the lower Mississippi territory along the Gulf of Mexico that included West Florida and most of what is now southwestern Mississippi. British officials offered large land grants to attract white settlers to the region. But even so, as West Florida's first governor, George Johnstone, noted, the colony's ultimate success would depend on African slaves, "without which," he said, "it will be impossible to raise the colony to any eminence."[4]

During the short period of British rule, which ended in 1783, not many settlers were attracted to the area, but those who did move in, such as those in the Natchez region, came to depend heavily upon slave labor. By 1774 roughly one-quarter of the population was African American, and by 1780 nearly one-third. After the Spanish took control in 1783, slavery in the Natchez region expanded even more rapidly, and the population became nearly 40 percent African American by 1790.

Slaves in West Florida were highly valued, since settlers estimated that slave laborers there would provide masters with more than a 40 percent return on their original investment each year. Nonetheless, despite the region's frontier conditions, its African Americans faced the typical restrictions put on blacks elsewhere in North America: limits on alcohol consumption, constraints on free assembly, bans on carrying firearms, and refusal of free movement. Here again, easy generalizations about the democratic effects of the frontier and its encouragement of the growth of liberty break down when all members of the American population are considered.

thirteen

The Native American Frontier

I boast that I am the only Negro in the United States whose
grandfather on the mother's side was *not* an Indian chief.

Zora Neale Hurston, *Dust Tracks on a Road* (1942)

From the time of the first Spanish expeditions of the sixteenth century,
Africans in the Americas often escaped from their European masters or aban-
doned European expeditions to settle among the local Indians. In part 2 we
noted that such black-red alliances operated in the Spanish-controlled territories. Here we will examine African interaction with the Native Americans in
the English mainland colonies.

Most Africans arriving in English North America were put to work in
regions where the majority of people were Native American. Thus, Indians
and African newcomers commonly found themselves living near one another,
and especially in the seventeenth century Indians and blacks were often
enslaved to the same master. Since the Africans imported into the English
colonies were predominantly male and the bordering Indian population, suffering the demographic effects of the European invasion, was predominantly
female, sexual relationships and marriages between the two groups were common and resulted in continual social and racial intermixture. A good number
of those African Americans classified uncertainly in colonial censuses as
mixed-race (mustees and mulattoes) were of mixed African and Native
American ancestry rather than a mixture of African and European stock.

Paul Cuffe, the famous African American ship captain, merchant trader,
and African colonizer from New England, represents this mingling of black
and red. His father, Kofi, an African from the Akan area of the Gold Coast,
married a Gayhead Wampanoag woman named Ruth Moses in 1746 and

settled in Massachusetts. When it came time for their son Paul to marry, the young man (who then identified himself as mustee) married Alice Pequit, a Wampanoag of his mother's people. Later Cuffe seems to have shifted his ethnic identification toward his father's heritage, for he became a well-known leader in the fight for African American voting rights and repatriation to Africa.

Another New Englander who was the product of such a marriage, William Brown, explained the trend by noting that "Indian women observing the colored men working for their wives, and living after the manner of white people, in comfortable houses, felt anxious to change their position in life" and so married African Americans.[1] The revolutionary war hero Crispus Attucks was said to have been the product of such a union. Moreover, relations between the two races were close enough in the North that both groups joined in the election day and the Dutch Pentecost, or "Pinkster," festivities celebrated by the region's blacks during the last half of the eighteenth century.

Sometimes the alliances became more militant, for both Indians and Africans had sufficient reason to see the English as oppressive. As early as 1657 blacks and Indians rose together in Connecticut, but the primary result was increasingly repressive regulation and a new law excluding blacks from the local militia. A generation later Boston masters made a policy of hiring Indians to hunt down runaway slaves in return for small bounties; clearly part of the intent was to foster divisions between the region's people of color.

Many of the colonies during the French and Indian War enlisted African Americans into their land and sea forces. They probably did so to augment their forces rather than as a concerted policy to foster hatred between Indians and Negroes, but from the black point of view, military service was a path to freedom. And even before 1763 many of the southern colonies had begun to fear the potential for revolution if too many slaves were given access to arms and military training.

In the Chesapeake area white officials had long employed Negroes in their military excursions against local Indians. But the tactic backfired during Bacon's Rebellion of 1676, when the poorer whites in the militia sent out against the Indians switched objectives and joined with black militiamen in a threatening alliance against the colonial elite.

Potential alliances between blacks and Indians were considered most dangerous on the southeastern frontier because the Indian nations there were so much stronger and because the nearby Spanish were always suspected of trying to foment trouble with disgruntled elements within the English colonies. Therefore, as a matter of imperial policy, white authorities in the southern colonies tried to include black troops as often as possible in Indian wars, such as the English aggressions against the Yamassees in 1715 and against the Cherokees in 1760–61; white officials also adopted the policy of hiring Indians to find and return escaped slaves and to attack "maroon" settlements—communities of self-liberated and independent African Americans.

As John Brickell explained in 1737: "[The Indians] are also very expeditious in finding out the *Negroes* that frequently run away from their masters into the Woods, where they commit many outrages against the *Christians*. . . . The *Indian* Kings are sent for on these Occasions, who soon find out their Haunts, and commonly kill many of them whenever they are sent in pursuit after them, for they never cease pursuing 'till they destroy or hunt them out of the Woods."[2]

Although whites did all in their power to divide red from black and thereby create lasting animosities that would prevent the peoples of color from rising together against the white settlements, the policy had only limited success. Blacks and Indians understood the similarity of their positions, commonly socialized with one another, and sometimes become allies in the struggle against the English when both saw an advantage in it.

Just such a shocking surprise awaited the expedition of Col. John Barnwell of South Carolina against King Hancock's Tuscarora Indians in 1712. The Indians whom Colonel Barnwell had expected to defeat so easily had built a solid defensive fortification along the riverbank featuring two tiers of portholes and reinforced by unprecedented defensive works, including a large trench backed by a high earthen bank. The approach to the fort was painstakingly laid out to slow and harass an approaching enemy: tree limbs had been cut and placed across potential trails, and brush camouflaged a bulwarks of sharply pointed canes angled forward to impale careless invaders. Barnwell was told that the unusual fortification techniques—common enough in West Africa—had been taught to the Tuscarora by a runaway Negro named Harry who had been sold away to Virginia for roguery but instead had escaped and joined the Indians.

Louisiana officials discouraged enslavement of Indians because of their fear that enslaved Indians would encourage the colony's African slaves to run away and develop threatening black-red alliances; as Gov. Étienne Boucher de Périer warned in 1728, "these Indian slaves being mixed with our negroes may induce them to desert with them, as has already happened, as they may maintain relations with them which might be disastrous to the colony when there are more blacks."[3] And in fact just such black cooperation with Louisiana's Natchez Indians led in 1729 to a joint offensive against the French at the new town of Natchez on the Mississippi, an onslaught in which the settlement was crushed and its inhabitants slaughtered.

Given such circumstances, it is not surprising that colonial policy generally favored using blacks and Indians as often as possible to fight or capture one another and so divide the potential allies. But this scheme, too, was not without its dangers, for using black militia to destroy the Indians might also have endangered the whites by, in the words of Louisiana Governor Périer, "rendering [the blacks] too bold and . . . inclining them perhaps to revolt after the example of those who joined the Natchez [in 1729]."[4] Nonetheless, French officials in Louisiana instituted a policy of using black troops, and African

American soldiers fought against Native American forces in the Chickasaw War of the 1730s and the Choctaw War of the 1740s. French officials also forbade white settlers who were going to live among the Indians to own black slaves and refused to let traders bring black slaves with them into Indian lands.

From the earliest years, when slaves in the Chesapeake area ran off into the wilderness, they often established small maroon communities by joining with fellow escapees from servitude, both whites and Native Americans, including isolated survivors of the holocaust-like decimation of the local Indian peoples. The most important of these maroon settlements were in the Great Dismal Swamp along the Virginia–North Carolina border. Although these Swamp communities were first dominated by Tuscarora warriors, by the middle of the eighteenth century Africans were the more numerous and influential. The multiracial settlements of the Great Dismal Swamp featured cultural interaction and intermarriage and were, interestingly enough, the best examples of multicultural harmony in the English colonies during the colonial era.

All across the Appalachian frontier, black men who had escaped from slavery were blending into the weaker Indian nations, who welcomed them as replacements for their own dwindling supply of males. The result was a situation like that in the 1780s when white Virginians agitated for the termination of the Gingaskin Indian Reservation in Northampton Country because there were few real Native Americans left there, the other "Indians" being, in reality, free Negroes who wished to escape white control.

Neither African Americans nor Native Americans have been given their proper due in the history of colonial America. Despite the efforts of white colonials to divide and subdue the darker peoples within their territories, both groups fought to maintain or reassert their own freedoms and, more often than we might suppose, struggled as allies. Looking at black-Indian alliances, we come to understand that the colonial struggle for liberty was far more complex and multifaceted than many realize.

Part Four

A New African American Culture

fourteen

New Ways in the New World

The idea that African-American culture is exclusively a thing apart, separate from the whole, having no influence on the shape and shaping of American culture, is a racialist fiction.

Henry Louis Gates, Jr., *Loose Canons* (1992)

Many Americans of African (and part-African) ancestry who are forever complaining, mostly in the vaguest of generalities, and almost always with more emotion than intellectual conviction, that their black captive forefathers were stripped of their native culture by white Americans often seem to have a conception of culture that is more abstract, romantic, and in truth, pretentious than functional. Neither African nor American culture seems ever to have been, as most polemicists perhaps unwittingly assume, a static system of racial conventions and ornaments. Culture of its very essence is a dynamic, ever accommodating, ever accumulating, ever assimilating environmental phenomenon.

Albert Murray, *The Omni-Americans* (1970)

In the colonial environment of English North America, Old World traditions from the western regions of Africa and Europe were fused and then blended with new concepts borrowed from the native peoples of North America and nearby colonial systems. The result was an unprecedented, and unintended, new multicultural American way of life. Men and women from Africa were especially affected by this process of amalgamation because, as slaves, cultural change was forced upon them. Still, "new Negroes" from Africa and the West Indies, finding much in European culture that was useful, willingly adopted or transformed it to their own needs.

Because of the rapidity with which Africans moved away from their earlier nationalities and became multiculturally "American," in a sense they were the first cultural citizens of our developing nation. Certainly African Americans adopted an "American" identity quicker than did their English co-settlers (or neighboring Native Americans), who were far more conservatively committed to maintaining old ways and customs.

For the black colonial population, the process of cultural transformation began all over again with each newly arriving group of Africans; the new arrivals had little choice but to adapt to new North American practices, which were themselves only just forming. This adjustment was not as difficult a transition as we might suppose: the cultures of Africa and Europe were both still dominated by the rhythms and sensibilities of a premodern, agricultural way of life shaped more by folk religion than by science, and domestic responsibilities were relatively similar on both continents. The greatest problem that black and white laborers faced in working together in the colonies was communicating effectively, but even this handicap proved a minor impediment to the creation of a new American way of life.

Clearly the success of the whole colonial enterprise in English North America would have been impossible without the economic and cultural contributions of African Americans. Nonetheless, because most Africans and black West Indians had come to the colonies as slaves and were held, with their progeny, to lifetime tenures of bondage, black Americans were rarely able to enjoy an equitable division of the fruits of their labors.

As the years passed, whites rationalized the unfairness of colonial servitude as a natural and necessary result of what they argued was the Africans' biological, cultural, and religious inferiority. Such differences had not seemed so obvious to the first generations of settlers, but by the late seventeenth century the white theorists were basing their beliefs on the circular reasoning that, since blacks functioned well in servitude, they must have been destined for enslavement. A variant of the same specious argument would later energize the American struggle for independence: colonials contended that if they did not protect their rights and liberties from British tyranny, they, too, like their slaves, would deserve oppression.

Such protoracist thinking led to the slow but steady development of an American caste system, a system of racial hierarchy that by the end of the seventeenth century had separated the experiences of white and black settlers into two interrelated but dissimilar realms. That growing racial divide made the slow process of cultural amalgamation and assimilation that we might call Americanization very different for the two principal racial groups that settled colonial America.

The growing separation kept the majority of colonial blacks in a milieu that was still strongly influenced by the traditions of Africa. Even so, the wide variety of ethnically specific African traditions carried across the ocean were being reshaped into a new generalized African American culture. The intragroup compromises worked out between Africans of differing nationalities combined with the external ones forced upon them by the alien white masters created something brand-new—the first truly American culture.

Ways of Speaking

You cannot understand all of [the slaves] as great numbers, being Africans, are incapable of acquiring our language and at best but very imperfectly, if at all. Many of the [American-born blacks] also speak a mixed dialect between the Guinea and English.

J. F. D. Smyth, *A Tour of the United States of America* (1784)

Tankè you whitè man, tankè you. Putè some poison and givè me. Two day and me no die.

J. Hector St. John (de Crèvecoeur), reporting on a Negro undergoing slow execution who thanked him for water and asked for death, *Letters from an American Farmer* (1780)

The process by which a new American culture was being formed is illustrated by the distinctive language African Americans spoke during the colonial era. Remember that upon arrival in the North American colonies, Africans from literally hundreds of societies were mixed together with little attention to their national origins; as a result, few new slaves found themselves living near a large enough number of countrymen to be able to continue speaking their old tongue as their primary language. Although many Africans might have been able to understand the language of nearby African countries, communication in America called for much new learning and compromise, especially since slave owners' commands, which had to be obeyed, were always given in a European tongue.

Most newly arrived Africans quickly moved from the simple improvised sign language of necessity to stumbling attempts to master the new language they needed to speak if they were going to be understood by whites and blacks alike. For the building blocks of the new African American speech, colonial African Americans took the basic working vocabulary of the surrounding white culture. This was a compelling starting point not only because of the external demands of slavery but also because the black community had an internal need to avoid what Gov. Alexander Spotswood of Virginia called in 1710 "that Babel of Languages" spoken by first-generation Africans. Also contributing to the quick adoption of an English linguistic core was the influence of early black arrivals from the British West Indies, who as experienced hands already spoke at least some English.

Grammatically, most new slaves continued to develop their syntax around familiar African patterns. The resultant mixture of a new English vocabulary with an eclectic blending of older West African grammars and pronunciation made intraslave communication often unintelligible to masters, who blamed the problem not on their own linguistic limitations but on African stupidity. Typical were the complaints of the Virginia House of Burgesses in 1699: "The variety and Strangeness of their languages, and the weakness and Shallowness of their minds renders it in a manner impossible to attain any Progress in their Conversion."[1] Of course, from the African perspective this conclusion was blatant nonsense, as the Mendi-born Ka-le would point out to John Adams in 1841: "Some people say Mendi people crazy, Mendi people dolt, because we no talk American language. Merica people no talk Mendi language. Merica people dolt?"[2]

During the colonial era it was not unusual for African Americans to be multilingual, and some spoke several European languages as well as their African natal tongue (or tongues). After their first year in America most new slaves were able to be understood, at least at the most basic level, in both the black and white dialects of their master's language. Certainly, in a linguistic sense, African Americans were far more cosmopolitan and learned than the European American elite who owned them.

By the early 1700s a Creole language later known as Gullah came into existence in the lowland rice plantations of South Carolina, where the African-born majority was relatively isolated from both whites and the highly assimilated urban African Americans of Charles Town. Gullah, as might be expected, retained much African vocabulary. In a similar environment in Louisiana, an Afro-French Creole based upon a Portuguese-French-Senegalese pidgin brought from the West Coast of Africa in the early eighteenth century developed in much the same way.

African Americans across the colonies reshaped the languages of their masters and their old homelands into what was recognized by both whites and blacks as a new African American mode of speech. While neighboring whites could usually understand and even imitate it, the African American language pattern was used primarily by blacks. This was not simply a question of the limitations of assimilation. Black English was also manifestly a form of self-identification; it may have been formed in the flux of cultural compromise, but African Americans maintained their speech through the years as a marker of ethnic consciousness, a clear symbol of the social separateness of African American society, which was forced from without to stay separate but, equally important, was also held together from within.

Blacks and whites lived in close physical proximity all over the colonies, but especially in the southern colonies that proximity reshaped the colonial English spoken by the region's master class into a variant tinged by African American speech patterns. It was typical for a visiting Englishman to complain, as did Edward Kimber in 1736, that Virginians were lax in letting their children "too much to prowl among the young Negroes, which insensibly causes them to imbibe their Manners and broken Speech."[3]

Noticing the influence of this interaction, some whites began to warn that living among so many blacks would inevitably corrupt European cultural purity; thus, in 1758 Le Page Du Pratz admonished his Louisiana countrymen "never . . . suffer [black slaves] to come near your children, who . . . can learn nothing good from them, either as to morals, education, or language."[4] But the warnings did little good, for American wealth had to be built on slave labor, which inevitably required proximity between black and white.

Indeed, a proper display of status required colonial elites to surround themselves with African American body servants, and in the southern colonies the richest colonials commonly used black nurses as constant attendants to their children. Little wonder then that by 1773, when the New Englander Josiah Quincy, Jr., visited the southern colonies, he noticed what he called "a Negroish kind of accent, pronunciation and dialect" in the region's white children, and he warned that white women were even more "vastly infected" by what he called the same "disorder."[5]

Receptivity to New World Ways

A new African American culture developed in other aspects of life besides language. How much a new slave retained of Africa or was willing to adopt from Euro-America depended on a variety of factors: age, class status in Africa, isolation from countrymen, job status, and the degree of interaction with whites. How much a white American was influenced by African culture likewise depended on his class and the amount of his interaction with blacks; the white elite and indentured servant classes of the southern colonies would have the most contact.

Few Africans over 35 were shipped to the Americas, in part because older men and women found learning new ways difficult; they were extremely reluctant to change. As the Rev. James Falconer explained from Virginia in 1724, those slaves who had "grown up before and [been] carried from their native country . . . are never able to either speak or understand our language perfectly."[6] Older slaves were simply unwilling to forget their African lives; thus, the London-based *Gentleman's* magazine cautioned in 1764: "No Negro should be bought old; such are always sullen and unteachable, and frequently put an end to their lives."[7]

Younger slaves were much more adaptable; they learned the new language with ease, like the boy advertised in the *Boston Newsletter* in 1759 as "about twelve months from the coast of Guinney, speaks good English."[8] Their natural curiosity made child slaves willing pupils of the new culture. Olaudah Equiano, who had been shipped from Africa as a child, explained that once he learned English and got over the crushing isolation common to those sold away from their shipmates, "I now not only felt myself quite easy with these new countrymen, but relished their society and manners."[9]

89

Class status also affected a new slave's interest in adopting the new culture. Virginia's Hugh Jones explained in 1724 that "those Negroes make the best slaves that have been slaves in their own country; for they that have been kings and great men are generally lazy, haughty, and obstinate; whereas the others are sharper, better humored, and more laborious."[10] Nobles knew little about agriculture and, like other rich men, were not strong enough to be of much use to New World planters. Elite Africans resented their new situations far more than did commoners or former slaves, who were used to hard work and low status.

As important as age or class in a new slave's acceptance of new ideas was the degree of separation from other Africans and the kind of work to which he or she was assigned. African Americans, like those in South Carolina, who worked in the fields in labor gangs away from most whites remained relatively traditional in their habits, while skilled black workers in urban settings and those in white household service more quickly assimilated.

New Families and New Kin

> Without scruple are relations and friends separated, most of them never to see each other again. I remember in the vessel in which I was brought over, in the men's compartment there were several brothers who . . . were sold in different lots; and it was very moving on this occasion to see and hear their cries at parting. O, ye nominal Christians! might not an African ask you, Learned you this from your God who says unto you, Do unto all men as you would men should do unto you? Is it not enough that we are torn from our country and friends to toil for your luxury and lust of gain? Must every tender feeling be likewise sacrificed to your avarice?
>
> Olaudah Equiano, *Equiano's Travels* (1789)

One of the greatest sacrifices that faced the new African Americans was the loss of the extended families that had structured most social relationships in Africa. The first African Americans had to make marriage choices without the traditional guidance and protection of kinsmen symbolized in the traditional exchange of African bridewealth payments—the valuable gifts given by a groom's kinspeople to the family of his bride. Such payments tied the interests of the two extended families together and ensured that the young couple had a support system that would help the marriage succeed.

In America bridewealth gifts must have seemed of little purpose, since prospective marriage partners usually lacked large families to perpetuate the tradition and young men, unable to accumulate much in the way of wealth, had little to offer. Nonetheless, first-generation African American families sometimes maintained the symbolic form. John Brickell reported the custom from North Carolina in 1737, and even if he did not understand very well what was happening, he did perceive that marriage among slaves was treated as an African-style social contract rather than the religious contract familiar to white Christians. As a result of the weaker family controls available to African Americans in the English colonies, divorce was common enough among slaves to scandalize Brickell: "Their Marriages are generally performed amongst themselves, there being very little ceremony used upon that Head; for the Man makes the Woman a Present, such as a *Brass Ring* . . . , which if she accepts of, becomes his wife; but if ever they part from each other, which frequently happens . . . , she returns his Present: These kind of contracts no longer binding them, then the Woman keeps the Pledge given her."[11]

At first, African American premarital standards seem to have been shaped both by those of the European laboring classes who worked alongside them and by traditional African customs, especially those that permitted relative sexual freedom before marriage or engagement. Thus, pregnancy before marriage was not uncommon among colonial couples, white or black. With marriage, most African Americans seem outwardly to have quickly settled into Euro-American–style monogamous nuclear families that traced inheritance bilaterally through the lines of both parents. Nonetheless, colonial naming choices show the continuing importance of African ideas of kinship among African Americans, for black children more commonly than whites were named after recently deceased relatives, a practice rooted in the African belief in rebirth across the generations.

African families, in contrast to their African American counterparts, were generally polygynous rather than monogamous and, for the most part, traced ancestry only through one parent's line—usually the male side at that time in West Africa. Therefore, traditional African families were larger but had closer kinship connections than African American families, since all cousins were related to precisely the same set of ancestors: in our bilateral system, our cousins have aunts and uncles who, though relatives to them, are not related to us.

Although outwardly the new African American forms of marriage looked like Euro-American ones, they were not the same. This difference stemmed partly from the white-dominated colonial legal systems not recognizing the legitimacy of slave marriages and therefore making black families extremely vulnerable to enforced separations. But other distinctions dated back to the Old World: whereas marriage was a religiously sanctioned institution for Christian Europeans, it was a social contract in much of Africa, as reflected in the greater openness of African American marriages to voluntary dissolution.

Involuntary separation caused by the sale of a spouse was a cruel American innovation that seriously eroded African American marital stability. In the end the combination of willing and unwilling separations created a variety of African American marriage relationships that even white observers recognized as different from their own. As the Rev. John Barrow of New York complained in 1725: "[The blacks] will not or cannot live up to the Christian covenant in one notorious instant at least, viz., matrimony, for they marry after their heathen way and divorce and take others as often as they please."[12]

In Africa much of a man's prestige came from his ability to support several wives and a large family. However, with Christian resistance to such a custom and an unbalanced colonial sex ratio among African Americans (one woman for every two men), only a few African males were able to continue maintaining several formal wives. Most other African American men who could find a spouse were forced by circumstance to enter into monogamous unions, although some also set up less formal relationships supporting other women and children outside of their legal families.

Slavery became more demoralizing as the population became less African and more American. For the Africans who arrived in America, servitude was a familiar institution. Most had had experience with some form of bondage in their homelands, even if most had been themselves free. In Africa slavery had not always implied a terrible loss of status, and it certainly had no connection with race. But in America slavery was becoming an exclusive affliction of blacks and was therefore far more demeaning.

To compensate for this loss of face, some men tried to increase their sense of masculinity and status through relationships with women. The prestige that had come with polygyny in Africa, where only rich men could afford many wives, remained a goal in America, although perhaps the reflected potency was becoming more sexual than economic. Consider Roger, a Virginia slave who hung himself in a tobacco shed in 1712, "not [for] any reason . . . [but] being hindered from keeping other negroes men's wives besides his own," or Cambridge, a runaway water man described in 1768 as, "so well known as to need no other description . . . has a Wife at almost every landing on Rappahannock, Mattapony, and Pamunkey Rivers."[13]

African women in North America did not seem to miss the institution of co-wives; nonetheless, they remained reluctant to adopt Christian monogamy, since it lacked the protections for women that were part of African marriage arrangements. Moreover, Christian-style marriage was especially unattractive because it gave husbands complete economic control over their wives' financial assets; in Africa each wife usually exercised control over her own property.

Slavery gave women the economic independence to avoid or withdraw from bad sexual relationships, except those forced on them by their masters; consequently, many newly arrived African women were reluctant to formally marry. The resulting development of a looser system of sexual alliances looked immoral to whites, who chose to record as legitimate only the formal unions they blessed—no matter what any pair of black lovers might have thought or known to be the case.

A majority of the newly arriving African women came from patrilineal regions, where a young woman at marriage would leave her family to go and live in her husband's village as part of his extended family; once there, her status would be greatly determined by the number of children she produced to expand the line of her husband's forefathers. In North America these conditions were significantly improved, from the woman's viewpoint. New brides were not necessarily expected to move in with their husbands, and more important, a woman's children were seen in the colonies as directly related to, and part of, her own extended family as well as being part of her husband's family. For barren women it must have been a blessing that social status in America was less significantly determined by childbearing.

The first generation of African women may have tried to continue the traditional pattern of nursing their children for three to four years while abstaining from sexual intercourse, but in monogamous relationships this custom proved much harder to follow. Importunate husbands without access to other wives and masters eager to wring a full day's toil from their women probably worked together to push African American women into nursing and weaning patterns (and, thereby, sexual patterns) more typical of Euro-American marriage.

The greater fecundity in the generations following the first may have resulted from a reduction in the period of postpartum sexual abstinence as well as from the more nutritious American diet and better health of African Americans born in the new country. Although young women being prepared for marriage and pregnancy could not be separated out to be pampered and fed high-calorie diets as they were in West Africa, the high birth rate of American-born mothers indicates that they entered marriage with sufficient nutritional reserves to ensure fertility. Nonetheless, the colonial era's high infant mortality rate suggests that the maternal diet may still have been lacking in certain essential nutrients.

One of the greatest changes in gender custom was the escape by African American girls from the grip of the powerful patriarchal tradition, commonly found along the Sudanic belt of upper West Africa, of mutilating forms of circumcision to avoid what was believed to be female uncleanness and untoward sensuality. How this change came about is uncertain, but there is no evidence that the practice of excising the clitoris and other external female genitalia was continued in the Americas.

Did the older African-born men and women complain about this considerable break from tradition? Was female circumcision, and its less mutilating male counterpart, discontinued in North America because the practices were seen as inseparable from initiation rites into families and societies from which the expatriate slaves were effectively excluded by separation? Did African arrivals from the regions to the south of Nigeria, where female circumcision was not practiced, influence other African Americans to reject the tradition? Did second-generation African Americans ridicule it as old-fashioned? Was the move away from excision a kind of feminist revolt against a painful and oppressive convention? That we do not know the answers to these questions clearly demonstrates the limitations of predominantly white sources in understanding the inner dynamics of early African American history.

Even while constructing new institutions and discarding old ones, African Americans clearly tried to rebuild as best they could the social cohesion once provided by the now missing extended families of Africa. African immigrants tried to duplicate some of the kinship and age-mate functions of society by forging close relationships with their countrymen and other shipmates from the Middle Passage. It appears that the second generation of African American children usually honored such relationships among their parents' acquaintances with the formal honorific terms "uncle" and "aunty." In addition, many African Americans treated both the blacks and whites who lived with them in the slaveholding unit as a kind of artificial kin, and certainly the nexus between them was far more than economic.

In North America many white colonials soon gave up traditional European village residence patterns to move out individually on the land, but African Americans, when they had the choice, generally preferred to stay together, whether the men and women involved were free northerners or southern bondspeople. Such communalism, although partly attributable to the slave owners' need to control labor, was to a greater extent a reflection of the value that Africans and African Americans put on collective living.

In West Africa kin groups gathered their housing together in large compounds that featured centralized open spaces devoted to social functions and collective recreation. Husbands and wives within the compounds usually had their own separate family quarters; each adult possessed a small individual sleeping unit and shelter where meals could be served. In such African dwellings chairs were uncommon, and in colonial African American housing the old ways were maintained: poorer bondspeople commonly squatted or sat on the ground or on mats in their own cabins.

The historian Rhys Issac has shown that in early eighteenth-century Virginia most slaves lived in clusterings of more than 10 people. In these quarters, as in Africa, black social life was centered not on the interior of the small dark sleeping structures but outside on the common space devoted to social functions. In the southern colonies, as in Africa, women swept this common ground clean as one of their housekeeping tasks.

In their daily domestic lives apart from their mandated labor responsibilities, the slaves who lived away from their masters retained significant personal autonomy. They raised their children, scheduled chores, prepared meals, mended clothes, and enjoyed their leisure, all according to their own tastes.

The homage African Americans gave to fellow slaves was based on African social precedents as much as on shared Atlantic and American experiences. African societies were extremely communal and mannerly, and at the heart of most African social interactions lay the obligation to reinforce family relationships. Until the American families had enough generations to extend themselves outward, fellow slaves filled in for missing age-mates and kinspeople. In Africa the elderly, who were nearer the ancestors, required special honor, and African Americans maintained a similar deep respect for the aged within their society.

Unlike white Americans, who for the most part came from the middling people and lower classes, colonial African American communities typically included members who derived from the royal, noble, and elite mercantile classes of Africa. These men and women were honored by their colonial peers, and even whites had to acknowledge the great personal dignity displayed by the black slaves in their households, even if they were often made uncomfortable by it. Indeed, slaveholder manners were more deeply shaped by the social sensibilities of the African American nurses who raised the children of the white elite than they were by high European breeding or the social climbing pretensions of the white founding fathers and mothers.

fifteen

Colonial Black Religion, Old and New

> She fully expected at death, or before, to be transported back to
> Guinea; and all her long life she was gathering, as treasures to
> take back to her motherland, all kinds of odds and ends, colored
> rags, bits of finery, peculiar shaped stones, shells, buttons, beads,
> anything she could string.
>
> George Sheldon, describing Jin Cole of Deerfield,
> Massachusetts (c. eighteenth century)

If Africans organized their social relationships around kinship, their societies
also depended upon the guiding principles of a variety of religions. Although
some of the new slaves from areas like Senegambia were Muslims and others
from central Africa were Christian, the vast majority of new slaves had been
brought up to believe in many gods and thought each people and region had
its own distinctive supernatural protections and evil spirits. As a result, most
newly arrived Africans were willing to recognize the power of the new white
man's deity who oversaw the slave trade and American bondage; the newcomers were willing to try to gain some favor with this powerful Christian
god, just as they had often taken up the gods of their neighbors into the supernatural pantheons of their homelands.

Survivals of the Old Religions

In Africa religion and family combined in rites designed to honor and propi-
tiate ancestral spirits, who had the power to both harm and reward their living kinspeople. Because these spirits necessarily remained behind in Africa,
most Africans in the colonies expected to return home after death to the ances-

tors of their native lands. Their children, whose families were American, transferred this idea of a spiritual African homeland into their own conception of heaven as a less geographically located hereafter where deceased kin would gather and oppression would end. This African American heaven, outwardly Christian in tone but in fact a blending of African and Euro-American ideas, was a far more congenial vision of the afterlife than the one Europeans had brought with them from the Old World, and white beliefs, especially in the South, would draw closer to the African American model.

Because death connected the living to the revered and sometimes feared ancestors, funerals in Africa were extremely important rites of passage. So it was with the first generations of African Americans. Early black funerals remained African in style and importance, divided between emotional displays of grief before burial and the dancing, music, and festive gaiety afterward to honor the dead, who had gone home to the ancestors. One old Philadelphia lady recalled local African slaves "going to the graves of their friends early in the morning, and there leaving them victuals and rum."[1] In eighteenth-century Virginia a delayed African-style second funeral was also customary.

Over the years black funerals throughout the colonies became more Christian in content, but at the same time white funerals, especially those in the South, became more African American in their displays of emotionalism. Indeed, Southern white Christianity would come to reconceive heaven as a joyous home hereafter.

Another area of cultural convergence was in the realm of religious magic. Belief in protective charms as a bulwark against sickness and injury remained strong in Afro-America even if knowledge of the African "medicine" that had energized such amulets in the homelands faded away. Since charms were also common among the whites, no one complained of the potential devilishness of these small fetishes.

In South Carolina archaeological evidence suggests that newcomers from the Congo-Angola region may have maintained a tradition of using magic clay bowls to cook the "medicine" of certain of their protective charms, for they marked many such ceramic bowls on the bottom with a cross-shaped figure—probably representing the power of the Bakongo cosmos—before throwing them into nearby rivers, perhaps symbolically to send them home to Africa.

The sacred use of chalk to mark off or denote supernatural power seems to have survived the crossing to America; although there is not much evidence, it is suggestive that in 1741 slave conspirators in New York took an oath of allegiance to their planned insurrection within a sacred chalk circle. Violators of the vows were expected to be struck dead by lightning. Lightning bolts were commonly interpreted as a carrier of divine punishment in Africa, and many colonial African Americans seem to have regarded lightning strikes in the same way in North America.

African-inspired beliefs in fortune-telling and the divination of lost objects or stolen goods also continued in the American colonies. These practices were generally acceptable to whites since they were roughly similar to ones based on Euro-American folk beliefs. Typical of the kind of blending of the two traditions that went on in the colonial era was the transformation of a West African divination technique, based on tossing cowrie shells, into an American gambling game called "paw paw" (named after a slaving station in West Africa) that was played by both blacks and whites in colonial seaports.

Oddly enough, given the witchcraft fears common to European and African cultures, heathen Africans and pagan African Americans were rarely accused by white Christians of sorcery. In part this oversight followed from a European misunderstanding of how black witchcraft worked. Visiting New York in 1748, Peter Kalm described black conjuration as "poisoning": "The negroes commonly employ it on such of their brethren as behave well toward whites, are beloved by their masters, and separate, as it were, from their countrymen, or do not like to converse with them."[2] Although whites mistakenly took such "poisoning" literally, the practice did not particularly worry them, because they knew from experience that, whatever it was, it worked far more effectively on African American believers than on Euro-Americans. Actually, what African Americans commonly described as "poisoning" was a diagnosis of unknown illness as caused by malevolent magic.

African Americans continued the African tradition of interpreting untimely or unexplained misfortunes and illness as primarily the result of unnatural and detestable human intervention, the evil product of another's magical work. In fact, as belief in the Old World's ancestral spirits declined, African American fear of antisocial human magic seems to have increased. Formal specialists in protective or harmful magic like those who practiced in Africa were rarely officially permitted in Christian North America, but the general African worldview about the causes of misfortune survived in folk beliefs about "roots" or "hoodoo," as such magic would later be called. And during the colonial era many African Americans became well-known practitioners of the magical arts, working for both black and white clients.

Medicine

> I have since met with a considerable number of these Africans who all agree in one story: that in their country *grandy-many* die of the small-pox. But now they learn this way: people take juice of small-pox; and *cutty-skin*, and put in a drop; then by an by a little *sicky-sicky*, then very few little things like small-pox; and no body die of it; and no body have small-pox any more.
>
> Cotton Mather, describing the Coromantee technique of
> variolation as explained by his slave (1724)

The great strength of early African American medicine was that it was holistic. It was not enough to treat the physical symptoms of an illness; sociological and psychological manifestations had to be considered as well. This protocol followed from a general African conviction that illness was most often the unnatural result of evil spirits or human malevolence. To heal a patient, therefore, required knowing where his or her social relationships might be dysfunctional. The resultant cures usually required both physical and psychological treatment in addition to magical intervention. Whatever the case, patients were not left in the dark about what was causing their illnesses. If the diagnosis was correct and timely, the antidote would work, or at least so the patient and doctor thought.

In the Americas most African American caregivers were not able to be full-time specialists. Whites reserved such professional occupations for themselves and depreciated black medical practitioners for lacking European-based medical training. Even worse from the white point of view, African American healers used magical rites to augment their physical procedures. Nonetheless, despite white opposition, black men and women commonly served as "doctors" within the African American community, where they handled most nursing, midwifery, doctoring, and dentistry needs.

These black practitioners, many of them female, were certainly as good as, if not better than, their Euro-American counterparts. In colonial North America it was African Americans, not Europeans, who came up with the first medical procedures that allowed protection from the scourges of smallpox and scurvy. When Cotton Mather was questioned by local physicians about the wisdom of adopting his slave's method of preventing smallpox, he responded angrily, "It is a Common Practice, and is attended with Success. I have as full Evidence of this, as I have that there are Lions in Africa. And I don't know why 'tis more unlawful to learn [from] Africans, how to help against the Poison of the Small Pox, than it is to learn of our Indians, how to help against the Poison of a Rattle-Snake."[3]

African American hygiene of the era was generally superior to that of white Americans, for Africans from the tropical forest cultures traditionally bathed far more frequently than Europeans and took much better care of their teeth and gums. Although African Americans tried to maintain these traditions of cleanliness, frequent bathing was often either inconvenient or impossible in the cold climate of North America; moreover, white masters did not recognize the need for such, to them, unprecedented cleanliness, nor did they understand what Africans would have considered the basic principles of dental hygiene. Thus, in North America, African Americans seemed to have stopped using the traditional African chew stick to clean the teeth and stimulate the gums after the first generations.

Christianity

This day died Phyllis a Negro Sister of our church: I hope she had chosen the better part. Her Husband Brother Zingo, upon becoming religious and joyning my church, had an earnest

Concern for his Wife and Children, and labored greatly to bring
her into a saving Acquaintance with her Redeemer; and I doubt
not his Endeavors and prayers were blessed to her saving conversion. She was brought hither out of Guinea in 1759 aet. 13
or 14.

Ezra Stiles, diary entry (1773)

With the spirits and old gods weakened by distance, the divinity who had the
most power in the New World was clearly the God of the Christians. African
polytheists considered it realism rather than heresy to recognize this fact.
Nonetheless, in the colonial era only a tiny assimilated minority of African
Americans became members of Christian churches.

White attitudes generally hindered black conversion. Some slaveholders
thought slaves unfit for Christianity; many more simply did not want to give
their bondspeople the free time necessary for Christian instruction. At least a
few resisted because they feared that holding fellow Christians as slaves would
be immoral. Even the whites who worked hardest to convert African
Americans were a major obstacle because most ministers judged the legitimacy of black preparation by bookish standards that were ill suited to the needs
of the mostly illiterate slaves.

Thus it was that in 1741 Stephen Roe reported to the Society for the
Propagation of the Gospel in Foreign Parts that his southern Virginia parish
included 15 Negro communicants, about 100 blacks baptized, and over 3,200
Negro heathens and infidels.[4] Even as late as 1772 Ezra Stiles of Newport,
Rhode Island, noted that there were "not above thirty professors [of the faith]
out of twelve hundred Negroes in town."[5]

From the African American perspective, the white version of Christianity
seemed far too self-serving. Why was there all that white preaching about
lying, drinking, theft, fornication, and disobedience when the more central
commandment about loving one's neighbor was overlooked? Blacks would
convert to Christianity in significant numbers only after black Christians had
revitalized the core spiritual message of Christianity: the good news that the
oppressed were God's chosen people and would be blessed in the hereafter for
their suffering.

Moreover, even when African Americans adopted a veneer of European
Christianity, they reinterpreted it to harmonize with African beliefs. Sin,
which was not important in Africa, was downplayed in early African
American theology. The devil, instead of being a Manichaean figure of
absolute evil, became more of a trickster in line with African religious ideas,
which generally rejected a simplistic dualism of good and evil.

Becoming filled with the spirit became the clearest mark of the African
American religious initiate, not knowledge of the holy book. Whites might
know the words of scripture, but they did not understand the soul, which
blacks saw as the heart of the matter. Thus, the distinctive African American

theological vision shaped during the colonial years must be seen as more than an imitation of the original white model. From the African American point of view, black Christians were recovering a message that had been sullied and misunderstood by less worthy messengers; they were also reshaping the style of worship to better fit the African understanding of spirituality.

For blacks, services without music were hardly worthy of the name. European Americans permitted and sometimes even encouraged black improvisational singing, but they tried hard to ban both holy drumming and dancing by their slaves, practices that seemed to them far too heathenish. In the end the powerful need among early black Christians to express their love of God through joyful emotional responses, shouting, and bodily agitation was so strong that it could not be held down; in fact, it expanded to help shape what became the central religious movement of the colonial era.

The famous Great Awakening from the stiff Puritan-style Christianity of the first settlers came when white preachers shifted their sermonizing away from cold lectures toward hot emotionalism; this change was greatly influenced by the energizing effect that the emotional black response had on the white preaching style. But only in the South, where African Americans predominated, would both white and black Protestantism maintain this emphasis. Thus, it is fair to say that, while blacks were being converted, they were likewise converting. From the colonial period onward, southern Protestantism was becoming culturally and stylistically an African American faith.

White ministers quickly recognized they could increase black attendance at services by encouraging singing. Having a soloist line out the hymns to the answering congregation paralleled the call-and-response style that infused most African and later African American music. In Virginia the Rev. Samuel Davies recorded in 1758 the artistry that resulted as "a torrent of sacred harmony, enough to bear away the whole congregation to heaven."[6] He was hearing the first North American examples of African American sacred music, one of our nation's most important indigenous art forms.

sixteen

African American Arts

The greatness of a civilization is judged as much by its arts as by any factor, and in this realm African Americans were to become the American masters. Chilled in the emotional winter of American bondage, the complex cultural inheritance of West Africa underwent a metamorphosis, reemerging to take wing in the colorful spirit of the African American arts. In the colonial era we can see the beginning of that process.

Music and Dance

> The *Negroes* above all of the human species that ever I knew, have an ear for Music.
>
> Samuel Davies of Virginia (1757)

> In music [Negroes] are more generally gifted than the whites with accurate ears for tune and time.
>
> Thomas Jefferson, *Notes on Virginia* (1781)

> The slaves were allowed the last days of the fairs for their jubilee, which they employed . . . in dancing the whole afternoon. . . . In that field could be seen at once more than one thousand of both sexes, divided into numerous little squads, dancing, and singing, "each in their own tongue," after the customs of their several nations in Africa.
>
> John Watson, on black celebrations in late colonial Philadelphia

Despite our stereotype of slave singing as mostly spirituals, African American singing in the colonial era was usually secular in content. Black work songs

102

daily carried across the fields and waters of colonial America, and on moonlit evenings and holidays songs of relaxation and good times could be heard. Since most black melodies featured improvisational lyrics, the trials of slavery received a wide variety of artistic renderings. But in the colonial period most of the songs dealing with slavery were not the stereotypical sorrow songs of the midnineteenth century; instead, black melodies were more often biting satires that followed the African precedent of musically commenting on and ridiculing improper behavior. As Nicholas Cresswell reported from Maryland in 1774, African American tunes were a "very droll music indeed. In their songs they generally relate the usage they have received from their masters or mistresses in a very satirical style and manner."[1] This tradition of aggressive musical criticism was ubiquitous among blacks in the Americas and would influence a wide variety of later American music.

Instrumentally, African Americans combined African and Euro-American traditions. African-style banjos, tambourines, drums, and rattles joined European-style fiddles, flutes, and horns (all of which, it should be noted, had their own African versions). Drumming quickly became less important than it had been in Africa because whites discouraged it, while European tunes and styles of playing were rapidly adopted. African American fiddle players played for both black and white dances and sometimes called the figures as well. In the colonial period most black fiddlers were described by the whites as "natural musicians"—meaning that they had been taught to play in Africa or by African American instructors. Doubtless they arranged the European tunes they played into a more African American style. The blending of African musical traditions with European ones created a new African American music that was the first truly post-Columbian American art.

On free days and holidays the sounds of banjo and fiddle would draw blacks together with a magnetic force. Because drums were discouraged, dancers and spectators clapped their hands, beat their thighs, and stomped their feet to give the beat. The African ethnic dances that the first generation demonstrated during holidays were quickly blended into more generalized African-American styles. Some featured the shuffling, counterclockwise circles of African religious dances; others focused on rings into and out of which the featured dancers jumped as spirit and energy took them. On holidays black dancers tried to recapture some of the pageantry of traditional African rites by appending cow tails to their backsides and added color by attaching brightly colored feathers, flowers, and ribbons to their costumes.

Often the dances reached what appeared to white spectators to be a frenzy of bizarre movements and stylized postures. For unlike Euro-American dancers, who usually followed set patterns and kept the back and pelvis straight, African American dancers were extremely loose-limbed and improvised their performances in response to the shouted encouragement of their audiences. The dancers' well-oiled pelvic movements scandalized whites, who, like the observer of a Pinkster dance in New York, considered them "most lewd and indecent."[2] Nonetheless, sprightly Negro-style jigs were often featured at colonial white dances, and black dancing contests created what would become known as tap dancing—dancers supplying their own percussive rhythms by dancing on a board.

Oral Tradition and the Black Worldview

Master visiting his laborers: "Many hands make light work."
Slave, raking up after two other workers in the hay field: "No, no Massa, not when you'r rakin' behind."

William C. Fowler, *History of Durham, Connecticut* (1866)

After having given his master all his good years of labor, an old slave refused an offer of freedom that would absolve his master from supporting him in the future: "Massa eat the meat; he now pick the bone."

Observation of Prince Youngey of Framingham, Massachusetts

In this white-man world you got to take yuh mouth and make a gun.

Paule Marshall, *Brown Girl, Brownstones* (1959)

Like their African forebears, African Americans continued to use their oral arts for educational and social purposes as well as entertainment. The majority of African American stories and proverbs were humorous and aggressively satirical. For sorrow was not the predominant reaction to social oppression, either in Africa or America; defiant satire was. Blacks were especially noted for clever metaphorical speech that made their critical commentary on white masters less dangerous to them than it might first appear, for whites often seemed unable to pin down the level of effrontery implied by what was said.

Ben Franklin recorded a typical African-style witticism that he noted was widely repeated: "Boccarorra [White men] make de black man workee, make de Horse workee, make de Ox workee, make ebery ting workee; only de Hog. He, de hog, no workee; he eat, he drink, he walk about, he go to sleep when he please, he libb like a Gentleman."[3] Was the hog a veiled reference to the white man? How could a white man be sure?

Such observations were enjoyed and retold by colonials of both races, but the basic point was clearly African American in perspective—as was that of a popular African American anecdote about an old white gentleman who called his faithful black slave to inform him that he would honor his years of service by allowing him to be buried in the family vault. "Ah! Massa," returned Cato, "me no like dat. Ten pounds would be better to Cato. Me no care where me be buried; besides, Massa, suppose we be buried together, and de devil come looking for Massa, in de dark, he might take away poor Negro man in mistake."[4] These two examples symbolize the colonial African American's ability to open-ly and critically assess the white man's inflated claims about a Euro-American ethic of hard work and Christian morality—by making a joke out of it.

When the churchmen in East Windsor, Connecticut, puffed on and on about the grandeur of the spire they had constructed after raising sufficient funds by subscription from parishioners, Black Primus Manumit deflated the self-satisfied deacons with a poetic observation that survived long after the pompous speeches floated off into the hot air: "Big church, high steeple, proud committee, poor people."[5]

Naturally slaves used their folk tales and songs to deal with the oppressions of bondage. Where African traditions had blamed the slave trade on white can-nibalism and black greed, African Americans more commonly told stories of kidnapping to emphasize to the black and white children who heard their tales that in moral truth enslavement was based upon the theft of human beings. Thus, Jeremiah Asher remembered listening "with feelings of unmingled grief when my grandfather related the story of his capture,—stolen away as he was, from father, mother, brother and sister." And the white abolitionist Henry B. Stanton remembered for all his life a slave song recounting the white treach-ery that had sent Miantonomo, chief of the Narragansett, to a cruel death in 1643: "In my childhood we had a Negro slave whose voice was attuned to the sweetest cadence. Many a time did she lull me to slumber by singing this touching lament. It sunk deep into my breast, and moulded by advancing years."[6]

Dress, Body Art, Hairstyles, and Physical Style

> Commonly wears an handkerchief on his head, according to the West India fashion.
>
> He had for some time before taken much pain in plaiting & tying his wool in which he had a considerable que.
>
> His hair in a cue, with an eel skin, but sometimes combs it about his head and shoulders in the form of a whig.
>
> [He has] a remarkable loose jostling way of walking.
>
> Eighteenth-century newspaper advertisements
for runaway slaves

In America, Africans were forced to give up the flowing robes and other tra-ditional clothing styles they had worn in their homelands. In place of these comfortable garments, their masters handed out to them cheap European-style clothing. North American slave owners did not permit blacks to appear in African attire except in certain rare holiday situations. Yet black Americans still expressed their own ideas about dress and proper attire. When season and climate permitted, African American children wore little clothing besides a loose shift or trousers, not just because their masters were stingy but because black parents thought more would be uncomfortable false modesty. Away from white eyes in the coastal low country of South Carolina and Georgia, black field-workers of both sexes often worked stripped to the waist during the summer, much as they would have in Africa, and their habit of going barefoot in warm weather reflected their own traditional sense of comfort even more than the unquestioned cheapness of their nominal owners.

For dressier occasions, however, African Americans loved Euro-American higher fashions, which had long been imported to the African coast as part of the luxury trade. For holidays when blacks had personal autonomy, they pulled out all the stops, mixing and matching the best European-style garments they could obtain. The assortments often looked as odd to white observers as did the imported ensembles worn by the African coastal elite, for the simple reason that the many ideas about style and color coordination that Africans and African Americans shared were quite different from European standards.

Because clothing is such an important indicator of self-image, it is important to note that throughout the colonies blacks were reported during holidays to be "very fond of dress," often choosing bold, contrasting colors to wear in eye-catching combinations that they set off with a variety of colored ribbons and appliqué. At such times African Americans commonly dressed so grandly that whites complained that it was unseemly for slaves to look so much better than their owners. As in language, African American style in dress was like, but not the same as, Euro-American style. It was more than a question of assimilation; style reflected values. In dress, as in colonial speech and religion, self-consciously African American cultural expressions were developing.

Both African American men and women commonly tied kerchiefs on their heads; it was working garb for men, but women used much larger headkerchiefs as a dress style as well. That their masters were required to supply such items, even though they were not an article of European American attire, is a significant indicator of the cultural resistance of Africans and African Americans to the aesthetic limitations of their masters' culture. What jewelry the blacks wore, such as their large hoop earrings, were also African in fashion. Interestingly enough, the typical "West Indian" male style that featured a tied headkerchief and hoop earring became the stereotypical garb of the pirate crews who roamed the Atlantic seas from Caribbean ports. Whites in the mixed crews had adopted African American dress as readily as they had patterned their sea chanties after their black shipmates' call-and-response work songs.

Despite the continuity from the Old World to the New of certain styles of dress, African Americans did not pass on to their children the body art featuring scarification patterns, which had been symbols of initiation, beauty, status, and ethnicity in Africa. They did maintain some of the hairstyles. Because of the tight curl in African hair, it could be shaped in ways impossible to achieve with the straighter, stringier hair of Europeans. Early white visitors to West Africa had been especially impressed with the variety of local coiffures: braids, plaits, shaved designs, and areas cut to different lengths were all common.

In North America, where there was less time for tonsorial artistry, most African American hair in the colonial era was cut relatively short, but women and girls often braided their hair into African-based patterns. Moreover, plaits held in place by ties were found on both sexes. Especially ingenious individual styles were sometimes achieved by shaping and cutting hair into shapes such as gentlemen's wigs; such efforts represent the freer, more improvisational African artistic style that can be seen in so many of the other African American arts.

Since in the colonies most blacks continued to carry heavy loads balanced on their heads just as their African forebears had, African American women possessed an unusually erect posture and graceful carriage, which included a sexier swing of the hips than was common among whites. By African standards of beauty, a fuller figure was most attractive in women, and African American women seem to have maintained this ideal in the American colonies.

Men set themselves off by adopting individual and distinctive walking styles, probably patterned at first after those of African chiefs, wrestlers, and master dancers. These forms of what today might be termed "styling out" were added to the looser and slower movements that typified first-generation Africans from the tropics; the result was an African American kinesics, a body language that soon came to typify the southern region as a whole and probably influenced the developing American pattern.

The Material Arts

Thou knowest Negro Peter's ingenuity in making for himself and playing on a fiddle without an assistance.

Isaac Norris of Philadelphia (1719)

The great wood-carving traditions of coastal West Africa were not successfully transferred to the North American colonies. Perhaps it is not surprising that religiously based ancestral figures quickly disappeared, for what ancestor would be honored to be brought into an alien land of slavery? Africans in the colonies sometimes created clay figures to honor the old gods, but in North America there were simply not enough people to sustain the old regional and ethnic religions. Therefore, wood-carving skills were used in the more secular work of creating spoons, drums, whistles, chairs, walking canes, and the like.

But the artistry that infused the mask-making traditions of the homelands had never been based on simply the ability to shape wood; the real greatness of the tradition was in capturing the religious vision—and that vision faded in North America.

Nonetheless, craft skills continued. In the southern colonies African Americans continued to make low-fired coiled and molded earthenware pottery and clay pipes reminiscent of Africa; in fact on some of the pipes they used decorative techniques—such as the *kwardata*, an incised diamond pattern on a banded background accentuated by white pigment rubbed into the design—from the Nigeria region of West Africa. As in Africa, pipe smoking was a habit favored by women as well as men.

African Americans also carved gourds for drinking vessels, just as they did in their homelands. But for the most part the craft skills of Afro-America served the wider colonial economy and were performed with Euro-American tools and techniques. Other African influences probably survived, such as the Poquoson-style canoes from early Virginia's western shore. Poquoson canoes integrated the natural curve of the wood into the design and in their variety of design resembled the multiple-log dugouts made in West Africa. In general, however, because of the limitations of current archaeological research, the record of African American–style physical artifacts is much stronger for the nineteenth century than for the colonial era.

Cuisine

> Under 40 years of age, can roast and boil very well, and understands made dishes, with baking of bread and pickling.
>
> Eighteenth-century Virginia sale notice for a Negro man

> In many families, Negroes had an important position, especially as cooks. As compared with the Indians or the Irish, they were epicures. They generally took care to know what they carried upon the table, being their own tasters.
>
> New Englander William C. Fowler, on black cooks (*History of Durham, Connecticut*, 1866)

Throughout the colonies blacks were considered the best chefs, even though African cooking of the era was relatively simple and few African dishes crossed directly into American cuisine. Their superior reputation was based not on their preparation of exotic foods or novel dishes but on their wider knowledge of seasonings and the greater zest they put into culinary pursuits. African American influence also made itself felt in the general adoption of certain foods that were relished in West Africa but little appreciated in Britain or Ireland. Okra, black-eyed peas, collard greens, yams, sorghum, benne seed, peanuts, roasting ears of corn, and watermelon all became staples of African American and southern colonial cuisine. And African-inspired pepper pots, hoecakes (called johnny cakes in New England), gumbo, and rice pilau likewise attained prominence as standard regional dishes.

West Africans ate little meat; what meat they did use they often cut up into small pieces to flavor stews or other pot dishes boiled slowly for long periods of time. Both Europeans and Native Americans were avid meat eaters, and in the colonial era African Americans changed their diets to take advantage of increased supplies of animal protein. Nonetheless, the original African patterns maintained influence in the southern colonies, where meats cut into small portions for frying began to replace the roasting of meats—which was initially favored by white Americans—in the regional cuisine. Moreover, the West African enjoyment of wild game meant that African Americans were much more adventurous than Europeans in adopting Native American food choices regarding animals like possum, raccoon, bottom-feeding fishes, turtles, and wild birds—items that most Americans would not yet eat.

African Americans of the colonial era generally preferred their own tradition of eating communally from large common bowls over the European practice of serving each person an individual portion to be eaten on a plate with a knife and fork. Diners dipped their fingers into the common dish, as they had in Africa. The custom for many African herders from the Senegambia region was not to eat during the day but only in the evening, a practice that prepared them well for the limited eating times allowed colonial slaves.

African dining choices, however, seem to have little effect on neighboring white Americans, who maintained traditional European standards in displaying and serving food, even when it was cooked and presented by slaves. It is possible that the southern plantation custom of using fly whisks to protect diners from annoying insects was an addition to the dining routine first suggested by African servants in whose homelands fly whisks had been in common use by the local elite. In any event, blacks who ate alongside whites were expected to adopt European table manners, and as the colonial period progressed, African American food customs moved toward those of their European American fellow colonials.

In cooking as in so many of the American arts, the African American heritage became a vital component of the new American folkways. Although European Americans at first wished only to maintain traditional European foodways, African Americans quickly changed their minds and, as cooks for both races, created a new American-style cuisine.

seventeen

Work and Celebration in the African American Style

Your country? How came it yours? Before the pilgrims landed we were here. Here we brought our three gifts and mingled them with yours: a gift of story and song—soft, stirring melody in an ill-harmonized and unmelodious land; the gift of sweat and brawn to beat back the wilderness, conquer the soil, and lay the foundations of this vast economic empire two hundred years earlier than your weak hands could have done it; the third, a gift of the spirit. . . . Are these gifts not not worth the giving? Is not this work and striving? Would America have been America without her Negro people?

W. E. B. Du Bois, *The Souls of Black Folks* (1903)

In colony after colony the white leadership asserted that success in taming the new land and making it profitable was impossible without Negro labor. The reason went far beyond African American sweat and brawn, although that was essential enough to sell out many a Christian slave driver's conscience. Equally as important, African immigrants carried with them an intellectual heritage, for how to do a job is often more important than the simple will to do it. In this chapter we will examine the skills that Africans brought to America before concluding with another gift, the great holiday celebrations with which African Americans marked their ethnic pride in a job well done.

Communal Labor

The Governor *Sir William* [Berkeley], caused half a bushel of Rice (which he had procured) to be sown, and it prospered

110

gallantly . . . , for we perceive the ground and Climate is very proper for it as our *Negroes* affirm, which in their Country is most of their food.

> Seventeenth-century Virginia planter, letter to England noting
> black expertise in rice agriculture

Africans brought not only their physical labor to America but knowledge and techniques that made their work more effective. African familiarity with rice agriculture, for example, helped create the first successful money crop for South Carolina. Africans knew how to clear swamps in preparation for rice growing and how to make the necessary drains from hollowed-out tree trunks. Just as in West Africa, Carolina rice production depended upon slash-and-burn clearing and gang labor to prepare the land, heel-and-foot methods of planting the seed, communal task work to tend it, fanner baskets for winnowing the harvest, and mortars and pestles to husk the gain. The successful production of this vital crop clearly depended upon an African-based technology and the labor skills of African American growers.

Most white Americans selected the plow as their farming implement of choice, but African Americans throughout the early Americas favored the hoe, which in a shorter length had been ubiquitous in Africa. Although hoe farming was more labor-intensive, hoes had the advantage of protecting tropical soils from rapid oxidation; moreover, hoes fostered the communal labor preferred by Africans and African Americans as a more social and civilized form of work.

Living Patterns and Housing

Guy & Jimmy [two slave carpenters] returned this day from Ring's Neck where they have been building two Negroes quarters 20 by 16 and an Overseer's house 20 x 16.

> The planter Robert W. Carter, diary entry (1768)

African American housing structures reflected continuity with African construction and design precedents but not direct copying. Outside of South Carolina and Florida, the few Africans in the southern colonies who built truly African-style housing with thatched roofs and walls of dried mud were mostly runaways living in maroon settlements; generally, African-style huts were too exotic for the tastes of white masters. Nonetheless, when black craftsmen constructed what outwardly appeared to be approved European-style housing, the foundation designs typically followed 12-foot patterns like those in West Africa rather than the paced-off 16-foot standard of Euro-American builders.

In the early years slave huts, with a single entrance, were usually quite dark inside and most often had an earthen floor. These features were very much in line with traditional African preferences, for dwellings in West and Central

Africa were usually small, earthen-floored structures of 10–12 feet by 10–12 feet, with no windows and only a single low doorway. Similar small huts built by the slaves in the English colonies satisfied the cheapness of colonial masters, who for the most part did not expect workers' housing to rise above bare functionality.

In the South, African American craftsmen working under the nominal direction of white masters also used African precedents and African American preferences to influence the white housing they built—beginning a long architectural evolution that would separate kitchens from main houses, radically lighten building frames, add roof coverings as structural elements, sometimes join buildings dogtrot-style, and expand the shading of front porches. From this African American adaptation of Euro-American architecture would eventually develop many of the basics of the southern regional style.

Black runaways taught southeastern Indians African styles of fortification featuring trenches, earthworks, and viciously protruding stakes, knowledge that clearly strengthened the Afro-Indian bands in their struggles against the aggressions of white colonial raiding parties. Whether European Americans also learned aspects of military strategy from the Africans who served alongside them in colonial wars is not as clear. Certainly African percussionists were recognized for their superior ability to beat out intelligible drum signals during battles, and from the Spanish expeditions of the sixteenth century on up to the Hessian mercenaries of the American Revolution, black drummers continually served with the white-led armies of the colonial era.

African-based skills were also especially useful in developing the colonial frontier. Throughout the colonies, Africans skilled in smithing and woodworking found ready employment. Black knowledge of cattle-keeping, canoe-making, small-game hunting, and net and trap fishing was essential to the success of pioneers along both the Spanish and English borderlands in the colonial Southeast. More important, African expertise in rice-growing, livestock control, and indigo production proved absolutely crucial to early South Carolina and Louisiana.

Horticultural skills from the African tradition proved useful in other ways as well. African American gardeners commingled plants of different heights in the rows, thus increasing crop resistance to insects, drought, and nutrient depletion and increasing yields. Moreover, African immigrants used their considerable knowledge of herbs and barks to experiment with the flora of the new land and thereby developed many useful medicines used by both black and white medical practitioners.

Since many African-based pioneering skills had close Native American parallels, Africans were probably quicker to adopt Indian techniques than were Euro-Americans; in fishing, pottery-making, and herbal medicines, African Americans doubtless combined African with Native American as well as Euro-American techniques. Especially in the colonial Southeast the transfer went the other way as well when the local Indians adopted African techniques and plants.

Sometimes African ways simply became obsolete in the new land. In West Africa experts in the art of memory won prestige and honor by keeping family histories and the communal heritage alive through skillful and accurate retelling of historical events. In the Americas print rendered such precise skills of little formal value, although many first-generation African Americans maintained mnemonic strategies and used them to recall important dates and family history. If such knowledge (based on African dating systems, which centered on important events rather than on calendar numbers) no longer provided a livelihood and important political position, it was still quite useful to the many colonials who lacked access to calendars or the knowledge of how to read them and so offered some blacks a route to local fame: "When members of the family applied to [Rosanna, a Gambian-born Rhode Island slave] as they often did, in real or feigned perplexity concerning the exact date of any past occurrence, however trifling, she was able to reply that it took place so many days before or after the time of the last (or whatever) Meeting."[1]

Probably other manifestations of these memory skills appeared in black oral traditions of the time, but there simply is not enough evidence to be confident as to exactly how such talents were used.

Black Entrepreneurs

Near [the Lower Market], constantly resort a great number of loose, idle, disorderly negro women, who are seated there from morn 'til night, and buy and sell on their accounts, what they please in order to pay their wages, and get as much more for themselves as they can.

These women have such a connection with, and influence on, the country negroes who come to that market, that they generally find means to obtain whatever they choose, in preference to any white person; thus they forestall and engross many articles, which some few hours afterwards you must buy from them at 100 or 150 percent advance. I have known these black women to be so insolent as even to *wrest* things out of the hands of white people, pretending they had been bought before, for their masters or mistresses, yet expose the *same* for sale again within an hour afterwards, for their own benefit.

A white Charlestonian, *South Carolina Gazette* (24 September 1772)

In their homelands many Africans, and especially African women, used the herbs they gathered and farm surpluses from their fields to sell and trade in local weekly markets where women were the predominant traders. Along the Windward Coast of West Africa female traders rose far beyond local markets to commanding positions in the great international trading enterprises of the region. When they settled in colonial North America, black women maintained their interest in local trading and market culture. The most remarkable—although an exceptional—example was Fenda Lawrence: she was noted in the Georgia Archives Deed Book in 1772 as "a free black woman and heretofore a considerable trader in the River Gambia on the coast of Africa [who] hath voluntarily come to be and remain for some time in this province" and who was given permission to "pass and repass unmolested within the said province on her lawful and necessary occupations."[2]

More commonly in the colonies, whites disapproved of black trading, and white authorities often attempted to inhibit black enterprise. The making and selling of pepper pot soup was an ethnic specialty that allowed some African American market women to support themselves in Philadelphia, but elsewhere small-scale capitalism was usually discouraged by law and custom. In New England, for example, city fathers tried to rationalize the repression of the Sabbath markets that had been available to black entrepreneurs on moral grounds, saying they attracted too many blacks away from church. In the Carolinas, African American entrepreneurship was discouraged nominally because slaves could too easily sell their master's goods along with their own.

Actually white businessmen had good economic reasons to legislate against their black competitors. Their real grievance against black enterprise was that it was too competitive. Small-scale white merchants could not compete with either the dedication or aggressive trading practices of black entrepreneurs, who were at that time mostly women. Thus, Charleston traders complained to officials that black slave women were being permitted "to cook, bake, sell fruits, dry goods, and other ways traffic, barter &c in the public markets & streets of Charles Town" so as to drive out white competitors.[3]

Throughout the colonies African American economic advancement was hindered because white businessmen discriminated racially and sexually in hiring, in choosing and training apprentices, and in lending money; moreover, white business competitors exploited the racial inequalities built into the legal system to reduce or destroy black business enterprise. Nonetheless, despite such stacked odds, colonial African Americans maintained a strong entrepreneurial spirit that only generations of rigged competition and enforced agricultural labor would eventually crush.

Since lack of capital was a serious handicap to Negro business, free African American businesspeople sometimes pooled their assets; indeed, the earliest forerunners of the later Negro insurance companies were developed in the colonial era out of corporate organizations such as the Philadelphia Free African Society. Members contributed initiation fees and regular monthly payments that after one year could be used on a rotating basis by members of the society who were in need. With the death of a subscriber, his widow and children became eligible for support. It is important to note that in addition to the insurance functions served by such corporate savings, these collective associations operated very much like the revolving credit societies of West

Africa and the West Indies. Thus, the black businesspeople of the colonial era developed their own particularly African American engine of capital formation, based upon African precedents but designed to solve North American problems.

Status of Women

> Sufficient distinction is also made between the female Servants & Slaves; for a White women is rarely or never put in the Ground if she be good for anything else, and to Discourage all Planters from using Women so their Law imposes the heaviest Taxes upon Female-Servants working in the Ground. . . . Whereas on the other hand it is a common thing to work a Woman Slave out of Doors: nor does the law make any Distinction in her Taxes, whether her Work be Abroad or at Home.
>
> Robert Beverley, *History and Present State of Virginia* (1705)

Both African custom and the economics of colonial slavery worked to give African American women more than their fair share of backbreaking work in the fields weeding, hoeing, and grubbing as well as even dirtier jobs like cleaning manure from the barnyards and building the dung piles. The greater expertise and experience in field labor that African women carried with them from their former lives made them far more valuable as field laborers than were the white females transported from Great Britain to serve under indentures. Unfortunately, this advantage became a curse, for black women's superiority as field-workers was quickly turned into a marker of caste subordination; white masters began to pride themselves on not making their white female servants work out-of-doors.

In America, as in Africa, the traditional domestic duties of child care, cooking, and cleaning were still defined as women's work, a double burden to be taken up after the official workday was over. To lighten their tasks, black women sometimes cooperated in preparing meals, much as co-wives might have in Africa. Black men had opportunities to take up more skilled labor positions, but black women were for the most part relegated to a life of constant drudgery by virtue of their gender.

Because the surrounding Euro-American society generally gave women less independence than was common in Africa, the status of black women decreased in the colonies. Moreover, the worst decline in female status may have been in the North American colonies. African American royal festivals in the Caribbean and Brazil honored black queens as well as kings, but in similar celebrations in New England and New York only males received recognition. Moreover, in none of the North American colonies did the economic independence of African American market women reach the level it did in Africa or the lower Americas, where such women continued to be essential.

115

Still, within their families African American women retained strong personalities and reserved the right to socialize the children they raised, both black and white. Colonial black women were far more economically independent of their husbands than were the white women who lived alongside them, and African American women were far less subservient to their mates than were their African sisters. Physically, black women worked as hard as men. They were proud of their strength, but their holiday dress suggested they were equally proud of their femininity and beauty.

Since fewer African women than men were carried to North America, the favors of colonial black women were highly sought after by a surplus of suitors and potential mates. Understanding their high value, African American women raised their status within their own communities to a level sometimes above their male counterparts, and within their marriages they enjoyed a higher level of autonomy relative to their husbands than that experienced by their white sisters—although this last benefit was more than canceled out by the insecurities of slavery.

Grand Celebrations

All the various languages of Africa, mixed with broken and ludicrous English, filled the air, accompanied with the music of the fiddle, tambourine, the banjo, drum, etc.

Henry Bull, on Negro Election Day in mid-eighteenth-century
Rhode Island (1837)

By the middle of the eighteenth century the northern colonies were developing regional variations of what was then becoming an almost universal New World institution—annual rites by African Americans in celebration of their royal African heritage. During these festivals across the Americas, black kings and governors were elected and then honored by grand parades followed by several days of feasting and dancing. In fact, in both New York and New England the white style of celebrating Pinkster and Election Days withered in competition with the rowdier and more amusing black festivals that soon dominated both regions.

In New England, Negro Election Day was far more attractive to the citizenry than the sober formality of early Euro-American public rites, and the region's white holiday celebrations and parade styles eventually became more African American in consequence. Outwardly, the African American royal parades of Rhode Island, Connecticut, Massachusetts, and New Hampshire looked like the Anglo-American parades that honored white governors; the black parades differed mainly in their raucous music and satirical style, the random firing of salutes, and the behavior of the surrounding crowds. African Americans were blending traditions of royal parades and secret society processions from across the African continent into a new African American style that usually included the antics of jesters in exotic costuming as well as serious homage to honored personages within the black community.

Similar celebrations, but without the royalty, took place in New Jersey and Pennsylvania, commonly during Pinkster and the day set aside for the general training of local militia. But in the southern colonies formal displays of black royalty, militias, or other officialdom apparently were too dangerous to be permitted. In 1795, when a North Carolina slave named Quillo ran for election as ruler of the black community, local whites arrested him for planning a slave conspiracy. In fact the master class of the southern colonies seems to have been the only master class throughout the entire Americas that was so frightened of potential slave rebellion that it would not permit holidays honoring black royalty or other mock officials. Nonetheless, the basic African American festive style, without the black officials, remained important in local southern celebrations.

Much from the basic African festive style was carried across the Atlantic to shape these newly developing African American forms of celebration. Music and dancing were absolute requirements. Traditionally Africans had celebrated far into the night, to avoid the stultifying noontime heat of their tropical homelands; this custom always annoyed white observers, whose cultural values had developed in cooler climes. In the same way, the noise level of black celebrations, customarily held out-of-doors, usually seemed excessive to Euro-Americans, who traditionally had to tone down their celebrations for life indoors. On the other hand, holiday drinking by blacks irritated white officials but was not viewed as different in kind from the consumption of alcohol by whites—only as more dangerous because it so quickly led to insubordination.

It would be wrong to think that colonial African Americans spent the greater part of their holidays grumbling conspiratorially over the daily oppressions of slavery or lamenting their sorrows in the mournful harmonies of Christian spirituals. That was not the African way. Instead, most black festivals in the colonial era were blatant celebrations of good times and featured what the Rev. Francis Le Jau of South Carolina called "feasts, dances, and merry meetings."[4] Holiday freedom was too important and too enjoyable to be wasted on sour reflection.

It would be equally mistaken, as many scholars have observed, to see African American festive occasions as evidence that blacks were relatively happy with their servitude. The best humor at black gatherings was usually delivered in attacks on white masters and their ridiculous pretensions; such assaults not only cut whites down to size but served to inhibit blacks from assimilating too much, becoming too much like their arrogant masters. A white observer of a South Carolina "Country-Dance" in 1772 caught the flavor of such black satire when he noted: "The entertainment was opened, by the men copying (or *taking off*) the manners of their masters, and the women those of their mistresses, and relating some highly curious anecdotes to the inexpressible diversion of that company."[5] In the same way, African Americans used songs, humorous anecdotes, dances, and folktales in America as they had been used in Africa: to reinforce community solidarity by openly attacking antisocial actions in the forum of social discourse. Such artistic verbal commentary was a traditional African form of resistance to abuses of power, and African Americans gladly maintained and expanded the custom.

Part Five

The Struggle toward Freedom

eighteen

"Til He Is Well Scraped"

Another unhappy Effect of Many Negroes is the necessity of being severe. Numbers make them insolent, and . . . foul Means must do what fair will not. We have however nothing like the Inhumanity here that is practiced in the Islands, and God forbid we ever should. But these base Tempers require to be rid with a tort Rein, or they will be apt to throw their Rider. Yet even this is terrible to a good naturd. Man, who must submit to be either a Fool or a Fury.

> William Byrd, letter to Earl of Egmont (1736)

He told us he invented two things, and by several experiments had proved their success: for sullenness, obstinacy, or idleness, says he, take a Negro, strip him, tie him fast to a post; take then a sharp curry-comb and curry him severely til he is well scraped; and call a boy with some dry hay and make the boy rub him, and unloose him. He will attend to his business (said the inhumane infidel) afterwards! But savage cruelty does not exceed his next diabolical invention. To get a secret from a Negro, says he, take the following method: lay upon your floor a large thick plank, having a peg about eighteen inches long, of hard wood and very sharp on the upper end, fixed fast in the plank; then strip the Negro, tie the cord to a staple in the ceiling, so as that his foot may just rest on the sharpened peg, then turn him briskly round, and you would laugh (said our informer) at the dexterity of the Negro, while he was relieving his feet on the sharpened peg! I need say nothing of these seeing there is a righteous God who will take vengeance on such inventions.

> The Virginia tutor Philip Fithian, *Journal* (1773)

Hagar, 14, . . . a Scar under one of her Breasts, supposed to be got by Whipping: Had on . . . an Iron collar about her Neck, which it is probable she may have got off, as it was very poorly rivetted; she is supposed to be harboured in some Negroe Quarter, as her Father and Mother encourage her in these Elopements, under a Pretence that she is ill used at home.

Runaway slave advertisement, *Pennsylvania Gazette* (1766)

The era of slavery was also a time of harsh controls, for no matter what the master class wished to believe about their treatment of servants, slavery was intrinsically a coercive institution. Each of the colonies continually adopted laws specifically dealing with control of their slave populations. Many of the early colonial codes, such as those in Virginia, Maryland, and South Carolina, were based on the harsh regulations originally developed in 1644 for governing the Caribbean island of Barbados.

Although the day-to-day enforcement of bondage in the British colonies was less ironhanded than the codes suggest, the master's will was effectively law. Moreover, slave owners could resort to a range of punishments outside the common law to reinforce their power. They physically disciplined their bondspeople with vicious whipping, branding, mutilation, and even execution; they sold unruly or impertinent slaves away from their families and friends; and they dabbled in a wide variety of petty cruelties such as handing out nasty job assignments, offering poor rations or ragged clothing, and refusing their slaves the time for personal social interaction.

Even many in the white leadership class understood that such unequal power relationships were in the long run destructive to both slaves and masters. Thomas Jefferson put it quite bluntly:

The whole commerce between master and slave is a perpetual exercise of the most boisterous passions, the most unremitting despotism on the one part, and degrading submissions on the other. Our children see this, and learn to imitate it. . . . The parent storms, the child looks on, catches the lineaments of wrath, puts on the same airs in the circle of smaller slaves, gives loose to the worst of passions, and thus nursed, educated and daily exercised in tyranny, cannot but be stamped by it with odious peculiarities. The man must be a prodigy who can retain his manners and morals undepraved by such circumstances.[1]

As bad as the psychological burden of slavery was for colonial Englishmen, it was, of course, much worse for African Americans. As the years passed, greater and greater racial restrictions were attached like metaphorical leg irons to those blacks who tried to pursue the basic human rights of freedom, dignity, and social progress. Consider, for example, the growing repressions placed upon blacks in Charleston, South Carolina. As its African American population grew into a majority, the colony adopted restrictions like those already in place in Barbados. To discourage Negroes from entering the city to socialize or trade, legislation was passed in 1712 requiring them to carry a pass from their masters stating their specific mission; 10 years later any Negro away from home anywhere in the colony was required to possess such a pass.

Whites across the colonies were constantly complaining that blacks gathering together in cities were too noisy and prone to gambling and excessive drinking; to put it bluntly, masters were disturbed by the idea that their slaves might be having a good time. By 1721 any black out after 9:00 P.M. in Charleston without a specific and sanctioned reason could be jailed for the night, and if such a person refused to stop and answer questions when challenged, he or she could be shot. In 1737 the law, strict as it was, was further toughened so that blacks on night outings were required to carry lanterns, to call attention to themselves, as well as passes signed by their masters stating their precise mission; violators of this ordinance could be punished at the public whipping post.

These laws demonstrate that the long-standing problem African Americans have with officers of the law, who hold a presumption of black guilt rather than innocence, started very early in our nation's history. Since masters complained so often about petty theft, their suspicion that some of this nighttime activity was illicit doubtless was well grounded. Of course, slaves often considered petty theft a matter of getting back property that in all fairness was originally theirs.

To reduce the sale of stolen goods as well as to reduce business competition, southern bondspeople usually were not permitted to sell merchandise or liquors without their owners' consent; they could barter with others only if they had written permission noting the precise quantity and quality of the goods to be exchanged.

Because of the danger of revolt, slaves were also not allowed to have or use firearms without their masters' permission. Drums, horns, or other loud instruments that could be used to call together rebels were also banned in many colonies. Typically a slave had to carry a pass when away from the master's home or face the whip; often as many as 20 lashes were prescribed for minor violations.

In some colonies, continual running away might additionally subject a slave to branding on the face or mutilation. Resisting interrogation by a white was a capital offense in Georgia, and the death penalty was widely mandated for arson, inciting insurrection, or for willfully injuring or killing a white person.

Of course, most of the offenses for which a slave might be punished were individual transgressions of a master's arbitrary and frequently changing rules, informal policies that often were no more than procrustean whims. And just as the master's rules could change from day to day or hour to hour, so too could the punishments. Consider the interesting letter that Joseph Ball wrote from England to Aron, his slave manservant who had returned home to Virginia in 1754: "You were very Saucy while you were in England, and Resisted me Twice. There must be no more of that; for if you offer to Strike your overseer, or be unruly, you must be tyed up and Slasht Severely and pickled: and if you Run away you must wear an Iron Pothook about your Neck: and if that don't tame you, you must wear Iron Spanaels till you Submit."[2] Ball knew he could not punish Aron severely in England without appearing a brute, and so he was reduced to making his threats after Aron was sent home. Ball's anger and the direction in which his imagination was running suggest a great deal about master-slave relations in colonial Virginia.

Even in the gentler slavery of New England, a slave who struck a white person, as Aron threatened to do, could be severely whipped. In Connecticut any black who even uttered angry words that might possibly defame a white citizen was liable for 40 lashes unless the court could be convinced there was sufficient justification for the impertinence.

To put the brutality of colonial slavery in context, we must remember that the British penal system of that era was nearly as ruthless in punishing whites found guilty of similar crimes. In the colonial era whips and stocks were used by English noblemen to punish their peasants; in villages such punishments were considered suitable for controlling local troublemakers, and university dons thought them appropriate for disciplining unruly undergraduates. English and Irish prisoners banished to Australia were commonly punished with floggings of 200 lashes and more. English marines and seamen, who were nominally free, received similar discipline aboard ship, and even unruly female convicts on Norfolk Island often received the "Botany Bay dozen": 25 lashes or more with a cat-o'-nine-tails while trussed naked to a torture board called the triangle.

For those whites who rose against the government, colonial-era penalties were far more vicious. Rebels convicted of treason, such as the merchant Jacob Leisler, who illegally took the governorship of New York in 1689, faced a horrible death: first they were hanged by the neck; then, while still alive, they were cut down and disemboweled so that their innards could be burnt before their faces; finally they were beheaded and their bodies ripped apart into four pieces before being displayed.

Thus, the cruelties of slavery were not designed as racist atrocities but were in fact rather typical of the brutalities commonly practiced by the British officials during that era to control the lower orders. That fact, of course, did not make such punishments less difficult to bear; indeed, as the years went on, blacks in the colonies became more and more victimized while treatment of the white lower classes began to improve. But in the colonial era it was not so much the difference in kind or even severity of punishment that distinguished black from white discipline as it was the arbitrariness with which privately mandated tortures could be inflicted on slaves by individual slave owners.

There was one punishment that had long been outlawed in England but came back into use in the American colonies to punish African Americans in particular—castration. Although castration penalties against slaves were severely limited after the middle of the eighteenth century, and not often practiced before that time, the Carolinas, Virginia, Pennsylvania, and New Jersey all prescribed castration for certain offenses, from habitual running away to sexual assaults.

Such inequality of treatment between blacks and whites created one of the greatest frustrations of slavery. Service was one thing, class inequalities were another; both had been accepted practice in Africa and Europe. What was new in the colonies was the development of a caste system that across the generations condemned blacks, and blacks alone, to endless servitude as dependent chattel slaves and left them virtually unprotected against the worst excesses that pyschologically twisted masters and overseers could invent.

nineteen

A Heritage of Resistance

As this is a time of great anxiety and distress among you, on account of the infringement not only of your Charter rights; but of the *natural rights and privileges of freeborn men*; permit a poor, though *freeborn*, African, who, in his youth, was trapanned into Slavery and who has born the galling yoke of bondage for more than twenty years; though at last, by the blessing of God, has shaken it off, to tell you, and that from experience, that as *Slavery* is the greatest, and consequently most to be dreaded, of all temporal calamities: So its opposite, *Liberty*, is the greatest temporal good, with which you can be blest!

The former Massachusetts slave Caesar Sarter, "Essay on
Slavery" (1774)

I learnt that Samba [Samba Bambara, commander of the slaves of the Company of the Indies in Louisiana, company interpreter to the Bambara, and accused leader of an insurrection plot by Louisiana slaves in 1731] had in his own country been at the head of the revolt by which the French lost Fort Arguin; and when it was recovered . . . one of the principal articles of the peace was, that this negro should be condemned to slavery in America; that Samba on his passage, had laid a scheme to murder the crew, in order to become master of the ship; but that being discovered, he was put in irons, in which he continued till he landed in Louisiana.

I drew up a memorial of all this; which was read before Samba by the Judge Criminal; who threatened him again with torture . . . upon which Samba directly owned all the circumstances.

Le Page Du Pratz, *The History of Louisiana* (1758)

As the story of the Senegalese interpreter and resistance fighter Samba Bambara indicates, opposition to enslavement had begun even before the slave ships left the coast of Africa. But once the vessels set out to sea, as we saw in chapter 5, uprisings literally became struggles for "liberty or death." Very few such revolts were successful, since most male slaves were closely guarded and seldom given time on deck without being chained. Moreover, African captives lacked the sailing and navigational skills to return their vessels homeward, and even if they had somehow defeated the Atlantic's stormy winds and high seas, they would have had no way to retrace their steps safely from the coastal areas swarming with African slave traders back to the countries of their birth.

Once slaves arrived in North America and survived their first few weeks, the shock and fear of the crossing wore off but not their anger over enslavement, especially if they were purchased by difficult masters. In North America, as elsewhere, resistance to enslavement was apparent from the start and continued throughout the colonial era, but in the English colonies, where the percentage of whites was far greater than elsewhere, African Americans employed less violence and more indirection in their opposition.

In the Americas as a whole, slave uprisings were so numerous that they have never been fully tallied. During the colonial era major slave rebellions were recorded in the areas that are now Santo Domingo, Cuba, Panama, Peru, Chile, Venezuela, Argentina, Uruguay, Mexico, Colombia, Ecuador, Haiti, Jamaica, Barbados, Saint Vincent, Saint Lucia, and Suriname. Between 1731 and 1823 Jamaica and Guiana alone averaged one revolt every other year. Minor rebellions were even more prevalent, and individual acts of resistance countless.

In the Caribbean and in Central and South America, where a geography of mountains, deep forests, or swamps permitted retreat and isolation, the self-liberated slaves known as *maroons* settled in small villages and tried to re-create the old African ways as best they could. The sanctuaries of freedom they set up became important threats to the slave systems of Suriname, Haiti, Santo Domingo, Jamaica, Cuba, Brazil, Mexico, Colombia, and Guyana.

The geography of mainland North America, unfortunately, did not offer early African slaves the same opportunities to escape into defensible maroon havens. Although small numbers of slaves would be successful in running off to nearby Indian settlements on the frontier more or less continually throughout the colonial era, their experience was not at all the same as that of the far more African refuges of the lower Americas, where some of the maroon states achieved remarkable autonomy.

In Brazil, Bantu-speaking former slaves set up what was virtually an African colonial state in Palmares. The threat to the Portuguese master class of this free black government was so great that between 1672 and 1694 Palmares was attacked by government troops every 15 months on average. During this period the prosperous Palmares state remained under the rule of an elected black monarch and displayed a clearly African culture. Similarly, in colonial Colombia the black-ruled Palenque of San Basilio maintained its independence for over 200 years, while in Mexico successful maroon settlements called *palenques* were set up near Veracruz and Acapulco.

127

Elsewhere Africans joined with local Indians to maintain their newly won independence by developing new interracial societies. On the Mosquito Coast of Central America such an alliance produced the Sambo-Mosquitos, an Afro-Indian society that was never fully conquered by the Spanish in either Honduras or Nicaragua. In Ecuador, as would later be the case among the Seminoles in Florida, runaway African slaves became Indian tribal leaders and successfully defended their autonomy from all colonial attempts to destroy them.

Certainly in North America the possibilities for both revolt and escape were far more limited. Slaves and newly arrived Africans were fewer, whites were more numerous, and the geography left maroon camps far too vulnerable to white counterattack. Most mainland slaves therefore had to try and make do, fitting their lives into the new culture that both they and their masters were creating. The most common forms of slave resistance in the English colonies did not center on physical violence, for the odds were too greatly stacked against a slave who tried to attack oppression so openly. Instead of a direct blow, slaves bobbed and weaved, counterpunching with a quick "now you see me, now you don't" strategy. Bondspeople resisted unfair workloads with purposeful inefficiency disguised as incompetence; they revenged themselves by setting "accidental" fires; they reexpropriated their own "stolen" property with multiple incidents of petty theft from their masters' stores; and they showed their general disdain for the entire system through drunkenness, disrespect, and running away.

Violence, of course, would have seemed a more viable alternative if sufficient numbers of white or Indian allies had been available, but masters understood such logic as well as the slaves did. After blacks and Native Americans rose together in 1657, the Connecticut legislature passed a law excluding all Negroes from militia training. The law did not lessen the threat, however, in the minds of northern white officials; in 1723, when Massachusetts legislators decided to strengthen fortifications at Castle William, they prohibited the stationing there of any Negroes, mulattoes, or Indians except those who were servants of the captain. Black troops at such a location, they feared, might be persuaded by offers of freedom to turn against the English and support an incursion by the French or Spanish.

That some of the African American slave population might defect to these potential enemies was not an idle fear or slaveholder paranoia. On the southeastern frontier black allies of the Spanish were continually sent northward to encourage such desertions, and maroons who escaped slavery by joining local Indians were known to fight with, and even lead, Native American units attacking the white colonial settlements.

New York City, because of its heavy black population, was haunted in the early eighteenth century by fears of slave insurrection, and in 1712 and 1741 local bondsmen were discovered to be prepared to strike just such a blow for African American liberty. In the first uprising it was recently imported

Africans from the Coromanti region of the Gold Coast who planned and led the rebellion. Meeting with several local Indian slaves, some two dozen of the new slaves (probably men with military experience in the armies of the powerful Akan peoples) coordinated a revolt to take their freedom even if (according to the confessions later extracted by officials) they had to destroy all the whites in the city to achieve their goal.

To prevent premature exposure of the plot, the rebels swore an African-style blood oath. Then, as a final preparation just before they were to strike, a free Negro (probably a religious specialist imported years before from the same area) rubbed a powder on their clothes to make them invulnerable. Such battle magic was normally used by African armies to improve morale, and apparently these African-born rebels considered it necessary for their own success as well.

On the night of 6 April, the New York rebels set their battle plan in motion. To disorient city authorities, they set fire to an outbuilding near the middle of town and then waylaid the whites who rushed to extinguish the blaze. Although they succeeded in killing nine men and wounding seven others, it was not nearly enough: when the local garrison and city militia responded more quickly than expected, the rebellion was quickly crushed. A few of the insurgents chose suicide over surrender, but 21 slaves were captured and executed—some were hung, others were burnt alive, and one was broken on the wheel.

Despite the failure of the 1712 revolt, and the decision to impose the death penalty for arson, another much larger conspiracy to strike for freedom was discovered in 1741 after a series of mysterious fires. The distortion of the evidence by severe questioning, which included torture, and a series of unfair trials under paranoid white authorities obscure whether this insurrection was the nonthreatening braggadocio of black race talk or an actual conspiracy to commit rebellion. Whatever the case, trial testimony led authorities to burn several of the African suspects at the stake for suspected arson and conspiracy to revolt. White fears were also inflamed by a series of self-serving letters from Gov. James Oglethorpe of Georgia suggesting that the New York events were all part of a larger Spanish plot that had long been threatening the southern frontier. In all, 14 slaves were burned at the stake for the 1741 conspiracy, 18 were hanged, and 72 deported.

A white New Jerseyan was horrified to hear an inebriated black man in 1734 boast that hundreds of local slaves planned to rise against slavery and then defect west to the Indians. Clearly the revolutionary fever had taken hold: the slave openly told the astonished white man that the English were nothing but a pack of villains and that he, a Negro slave, "was as good a Man as himself, and that in a little Time he should be convinced of it."[1] The alarm was sounded, and a number of slave conspirators were arrested; some of the accused were whipped, others had their ears cut off, and two were sentenced to hang (although one—the original leak about the rebellion—escaped).

Since rebels could not seize freedom in large centers of white population, black defectors throughout the colonies had long been following the basic frontier strategy of escape to the Indians. In the upper South runaway slaves usually tried to reach maroon groups hiding out in the difficult terrain of Virginia's Great Dismal Swamp or in the wilderness of the Blue Ridge Mountains. The Maryland Assembly in 1725 complained that slaves there often escaped to settle with the Shewan Indians, who welcomed them. To discourage such actions, Maryland officials punished the runaways they caught by cutting off one of their ears and branding them on the chin with an *R*. Despite such punishments, additional maroon settlements were reported in Maryland in 1728 and 1729.

In 1729 the English sent an Indian-led expedition after some 300 blacks who had settled in a maroon camp along the edge of the Chesapeake frontier whose members offered sanctuary to runaways and raided local plantations. Two dozen freedom fighters from this black band were captured and subsequently hung for the crime of "conspiring against their masters."[2]

Certainly, among themselves, slaves often spoke of their dreams of rising up and overthrowing the whites in violent revolution. However, most such discussion was angry talk rather than serious plotting, since the odds were so much in the white slaveholders' favor. Still, in addition to the New York uprising, large-scale slave conspiracies were ferreted out and punished in Virginia and Maryland in 1710, 1739, and 1740.

The conspiracy in St. Paul's Parish, Maryland, is the best documented of this group. The rebels were to be under the command of Jack Ransom, probably a native-born African American, but most of his fellow conspirators were new Africans who reportedly planned the strategy in their own language. The rebels hoped to initiate the rebellion with a force of 200 slaves and move on to unify both Maryland shores as free territory under a larger army gathered from the nearby estates. However, the revolt never got off the ground, and since only Ransom was executed, this conspiracy, like most of the others, may have been more a product of the fevered imaginations of frightened white slaveholders than the failed battle plan of an army of bellicose black slaves.

The most important, and deadliest, of the early slave revolts was the rebellion that began along the Stono River southwest of Charleston, South Carolina, in 1739. A group of 20 slaves, including a number of recent arrivals from Angola, under the leadership of a man named Jemmy apparently timed their insurrection to take advantage of the expected war between England and Spain (the War of Jenkins' Ear) which had just begun. Probably the plans were rushed forward in anticipation of a new law that white men in the colony would be required to carry guns to church starting at the end of the month. At any rate, just before daylight on Sunday, September 9, the rebels broke into a store and took guns and executed the owner before heading south to Georgia on their way to Saint Augustine, where they had every expectation of being well received by the Spanish authorities.

In their drive southward the rebels burned and plundered plantations. Their revolt was not a racial war, but a struggle for liberation. The rebel army spared the white innkeeper of Wallace's Tavern because he was known by them to be a good man and kind to his slaves. Another plantation owner endangered by the advancing army was hidden by his own bondspeople so that he would not be killed. The insurgents encouraged slaves from the plantations they liberated to join them; those who declined were forced into the rapidly growing rebel army anyway so that the alarm could not be spread.

The rebels rapidly marched southward under a flag of their own design and a rallying cry of "Liberty!" In the late afternoon the troops halted in a large field where war drums, which must have been made for the occasion and hidden until the uprising, began to beat out a series of war dances to rally the area's African population to the army. Apparently the rebel brigade of between 60 and 100 self-liberated slaves planned to cross the Edisto River after they had gathered into their army all the local bondspeople who wished to escape. It was a fatal mistake, although an honorable one.

Warned by a chance encounter with the approaching rebel army, white authorities quickly formed a militia from among the planters, who were always prepared for precisely this eventuality, and this larger, better-armed military force struck the insurgent camp long before the rebels had expected the whites to organize a counterattack. The result was a quick planter victory. Some 20 whites had been killed during the insurrection, and counting the rebels who were executed after their surrender, some 30 blacks also died.

Stono was a small revolt by the standards of the lower Americas, but it was large and frightening to the masters in the English colonies. In the aftermath, South Carolina authorities tried to ease their worries by increasing restrictions on the area's slave population, including measures that discouraged blacks from raising their own food, earning their own money, or even teaching themselves to read and write. White officials also tried to restrict the growth of the free black population in Carolina and set up heavy taxes to discourage the importation of new Africans, both groups being considered dangerous to the survival of South Carolina slavery.

In Louisiana during the hot July of 1776, a white plantation owner made a wager with several of his fellows that his slaves could turn out more barrel staves in a week of work than could theirs. Clearly this was a master who was proud of the competence of his slaves as workers yet had no respect for them as men. The arbitrary work speedup quickly led to slave grumbling and threats of a revolt, which ended when the purported leader of the suspected conspiracy was trussed up, thrown into a canoe, and set adrift on the river. This good worker died after he turned over the canoe, choosing suicide to a slow execution under the relentless sun. It was all so pointless. But it should have been warning of the frustrations that were building and would eventually lead to the far larger slave conspiracy that developed in Louisiana at Pointe Coupée in 1795.

Despite, or perhaps because of, increasing white vigilance and repression, slave unrest boiled up in new forms as the American crisis with Great Britain heated the countryside with debates on liberty and oppression. In Charleston slaves watched Stamp Act protesters parade the city to cries of "Liberty!" and then took up the rallying cry as their own, much to the horror of the white authorities, who tried to convince themselves it was only "thoughtless imitation."[3]

Moreover, during the upheaval over the Stamp Act, many slaves in South Carolina and Georgia acted for their own liberty by running off to form maroon colonies in places where forbidding swampland still permitted escape and isolation. Just such a group of self-liberated ex-slaves, including women and children, hid out to the north of the Savannah River and raided nearby plantations from 1763 until 1772; twice in those years white militia companies were sent into the swamps after them. In 1766, when a similar group of South Carolina slaves escaped during the Christmas holidays, white officials called in Catawba Indians as bounty hunters, the Indians being extremely efficient at tracking runaways.

White colonials had long feared that, in case of war with Spain, their slaves might ally themselves with the Spanish invaders. Now, as trouble with England increased, they worried that their slaves, who had heard reports of the 1772 Somerset legal decision challenging slavery in the English homeland, would strike for freedom as soon as English troops arrived. James Madison warned that the British might be expected to take advantage of such black initiative.

> If America & Britain should come to a hostile rupture I am afraid an insurrection among the slaves will be promoted. In one of our Counties lately a few of those unhappy wretches met together and chose a leader who was to conduct them when the English troops should arrive— which they foolishly thought would be very soon—and that by revolting to them they should be rewarded with their freedom.[4]

Certainly during the Revolution, far more than would be the case nearly a century later during the Civil War, rumors of war and impending emancipation ignited hundreds of local slave conspiracies intended to fulfill the principles of revolutionary freedom by expanding their application to black colonials as well as white. During the passions of 1775, for example, the presence of increased patrols was not enough to stop the plotting of slaves under the leadership of a bondsman named Merrick in Wilmington, North Carolina. Although Merrick's revolt was quashed by white authorities before it ever got off the ground, according to the torture-forced confessions Wilmington blacks and their allies from Beaufort, Pitt, and Craven Counties were planning a common insurrection with the intent of burning their way, plantation by plantation, to the British lines and independence.

When in late 1775 Virginia's Lord Dunmore formally offered freedom to all slaves who joined the British forces, horrified white authorities in Maryland tried to cut off all communications between Loyalist areas and their own slaves. Rapidly forced to take more direct measures, however, they disarmed local blacks of "about eighty guns, some bayonets, swords, etc." to prevent revolt.[5]

A year later Saint Bartholomew Parish, South Carolina, was the scene of another conspiracy. What was interesting in this instance was not that the plotters intended a general insurrection but that the rebels were led by several black preachers, two of whom were women. According to later testimony, the uprising was planned at religious gatherings held illegally during the hours of darkness; the rebels defended their right to strike on the religious grounds that white authorities were sinfully disregarding their servants' God-given right to liberty. The black preachers explained that the rising would be a new exodus under clear biblical authority.

Patriot leaders became so frightened by the 200 blacks who were massing on nearby Tybee Island and attempting to escape to the British forces that they made plans to peremptorily massacre all of them as an example to other slaves who might wish to flee. And to doubly serve their purposes, they intended to employ Creek Indians to undertake the assault so as to increase the hatred between the two groups while absolving themselves of the excesses. History does not record whether the attack was ever carried out, but the plans clearly reflect the white revolutionaries' design to discourage liberation movements among their own bondspeople and to weaken the potential for alliances between Native and African Americans in South Carolina.

The situation was not much different in the northern colonies. When the Revolution began, there were Negroes in Massachusetts who claimed to be ready to support the enemy, just as their masters had always feared. A group of Boston slaves who petitioned Gen. Thomas Gage for weapons reported that a great number of the colony's blacks would fight for him and the Loyalist cause if he would only arm them and then set them free when victory was achieved. Similarly, an escaped slave who named himself Colonel Tye led a band of guerrilla fighters against patriot famers in northern New Jersey for five years before dying from wounds in 1780.

The historian Sylvia Frey has discovered that in the southern colonies as well black groups continually applied to the British for weapons in return for which they would fight as Loyalists against slaveholders who supported the rebel cause. As these cases suggest, there clearly were Americans on both sides of the revolutionary struggle who were fighting for the cause of freedom and whose watchwords could be "liberty or death."

It has been estimated that in the lower South as many as one-quarter of the slave population escaped to British lines, ran off to join relatives, or attempted to pass as freedmen in the relative obscurity of the larger cities. The war also led to improvement in conditions for those left behind: slaves achieved greater autonomy over their daily lives after white militiamen were called up. Moreover, masters had to promise their slaves better treatment to keep those remaining behind at home. In both the North and upper South such promises often included pledges of eventual freedom.

Unfortunately, the British, despite all their noble promises to their black allies, treated them little better than did the patriots. For instance, although British Commander-in-Chief Sir Henry Clinton promised both freedom and choice of occupation to the slaves who escaped to British lines in 1779, by 1780 he was returning slave runaways to their owners so as not to offend Loyalist sympathizers. Moreover, many of the slaves who escaped to British lines were impressed as military laborers or body servants; others were forced, as if they were still enslaved, to engage in agricultural field labor to produce crops for the British army and Loyalist supporters.

For African Americans on both sides of the revolutionary struggle, the War of Independence was far more about freedom than it was for the many white patriots and Loyalists fighting for property and homeland. As the historian Benjamin Quarles explained: "The Negro's role in the Revolution can best be understood by realizing that his major loyalty was not to a place nor to a people, but to a principle. Insofar as he had freedom of choice, he was likely to join the side that made him the quickest and best offer in terms of those 'unalienable rights' of which Mr. Jefferson had spoken. Whoever invoked the image of liberty, be he American or British, could count on a ready response from the blacks."[6]

Just as colonial historians have considered early white insurgencies such as Bacon's, Culpepper's, Leisler's, Coode's, and the anti-Andros rebellions as prologue to the American Revolution, we should see eighteenth-century African American insurgencies as part of the same basic struggle for individual liberty and democratic equality. Certainly such battles for freedom were in the minds of the white revolutionaries of 1776 when they argued that their own right to resist "enslavement" justified them in severing their relationship with Great Britain. Manifestly, there is more to the understanding of the colonial freedom struggles than we have thus far realized.

twenty

From Revolution to Partial Emancipation

Sir, The efforts made by the legislative of this province in their last session to free themselves from slavery, gave us, who are in that deplorable state, a high degree of satisfaction. We expect great things from men who have made such a noble stand against the designs of their *fellow-men* to enslave them.

> Peter Bestes, Sambo Freeman, Felix Holbrook, and Chester Joie of Boston, freedom petition (20 April 1773)

We have endeavoured rightly to understand what is our Right, and what is our Duty, and can never be convinced that we were made to be Slaves. Altho God almighty may justly lay this, and more upon us, yet we deserve it not, from the hands of Men. We are impatient under the grievous Yoke, but our Reason teaches us that it is not best for us to use violent measures, to cast it off; we are also convinced, that we are unable to extricate ourselves from our abject State; but we think we may with the greatest Propriety look up to your Honours, (who are the fathers of the People) for Relief. And we not only groan under our own burden, but with concern, & Horror, look forward, & contemplate, the miserable Condition of our Children, who are training up, and kept in Preparation, for a like State of Bondage, and Servitude. We beg leave to submit, to your Honours serious Consideration, whether it is consistent with the present Claims, of the united States, to hold so many Thousands, of the Race of Adam, our Common Father, in perpetual Slavery.

> Freedom petition of several Connecticut slaves (1779)

Despite the liberating ideology of the American Revolution and its radical assertion of the natural rights of all men, most American slaves were not able to take their freedom with the founding of the new nation. When George Washington assumed the presidency in 1789, attended in his preparations by seven of his own slaves, all but two of the original thirteen colonies still recognized chattel slavery as a legal institution. And although by 1790 there were nearly 60,000 free blacks in the United States, the slave population of the new nation was vastly larger at nearly 700,000 souls, nearly 20 percent of the entire population (see table 20.1). That the new government, on breaking from Great Britain—where slavery was banned—decided to constitute itself so that one of every five Americans remained in lifetime bondage surely makes a mockery of any interpretation of the American Revolution as a freedom struggle. Indeed, it seems far fairer to characterize the new republic as a bastion of slavery than a land of liberty.

Still, the ideology of the Revolution had not been without impact. In New England progress was made in the revolutionary era toward applying the principles of freedom to all citizens regardless of race. In the northernmost colonies, where slavery was not considered an economic necessity, the ideology of the American revolutionary struggle reinforced a growing uneasiness with the propriety of men owning their fellow men. As Abigail Adams complained in a letter to her husband in 1774, "[Slavery] always appeared a most iniquitous scheme to me—to fight ourselves for what we are daily robbing and plundering from those who have as good a right to freedom as we have."[1]

This disquiet among some northern whites soon gave greater power to the ongoing petitions of blacks for emancipation. But popularly based legislatures were unable to take quick action on such a divisive social and economic issue. The deadlock was broken only when individual African American citizens brought their cases before the courts. In 1781 and 1783, Massachusetts Supreme Court rulings on the freedom of the former slave Quok Walker suggested that slavery might be ended on the basis of the natural rights arguments taken from revolutionary ideology; nonetheless, the court's decision was not publicized, and slaves continued to be sold in the state. Elizabeth Freeman, an ancestor of W. E. B. Du Bois, along with a fellow slave named Brom expanded the offensive by successfully suing for freedom in Berkshire County. Although the Massachusetts legislature passed no formal emancipation bill, public and judicial opinion quickly killed slavery in the state once the courts' precedent-setting decisions became more widely known.

The Elizabeth Freeman case is especially interesting because it gives clear insight into the African American side of the issue. Freeman, whose parents had arrived as slaves from Africa, was born in New York and (at six months of age) was separated from her parents along with her sister. She grew up in the household of Colonel Ashley of Sheffield, Massachusetts, where she became known in adulthood as Mum Bett, the title Mum suggesting her role as a nursemaid and midwife. Following 40 years of service, Bett liberated herself in 1781 after her mistress struck her with a heated kitchen shovel while she

TABLE 20.1
Black Population in North America in 1790

State	Slaves	Free	Total
Maine		536	536
New Hampshire	157	630	787
Vermont		269	269
Massachusetts		5,369	5,369
Rhode Island	958	3,484	4,442
Connecticut	2,648	2,771	5,419
New York	21,193	4,682	25,875
New Jersey	11,423	2,762	14,185
Pennsylvania	3,707	6,531	10,238
Delaware	8,887	3,899	12,786
Maryland	103,036	8,043	111,079
Virginia	292,627	12,866	305,493
North Carolina	100,783	5,041	105,824
South Carolina	107,094	1,801	108,895
Georgia	29,264	398	29,662
Kentucky	12,430	114	12,544
Tennessee	3,417	361	3,778
Subtotal	697,624	59,557	757,181
Florida[a]			500
Louisiana[a]	21,000	2,200	23,200
Texas[a]			600
California			165
Total	718,624	61,757	781,646

[a] Approximate figure.

Source: United States, Bureau of the Census, *Negro Population in the United States, 1790–1915* (New York, 1968), 57.

was trying to protect her sister from Mrs. Ashley's wrath. Mum Bett immediately left the house and refused to return. When Colonel Ashley tried to reclaim her as his slave, she hired a lawyer, claiming that under the new state Bill of Rights, about which she had heard while waiting table, she was born free and equal; as she saw it, since she was not a dumb beast, she must clearly be a free woman of Massachusetts, with all the rights of a citizen.

After successfully defending her independence in court, Mum Bett took the name Elizabeth Freeman to indicate her new status and went on to serve for

wages in her lawyer's household for much of the rest of her life. It was not service or hard work that had bothered Elizabeth Freeman; she was proud of her
occupational skills and her dedication. She simply would no longer tolerate a
lack of respect for her rights as a human being and fellow citizen.

Unlike Massachusetts, where the question of slavery dragged on into the
1780s, in Vermont the new constitution of 1777 explicitly banned slavery.
New Hampshire, on the other hand, went through a period of uncertain transition. As early as 1779, 19 slaves petitioned the legislature for freedom based
upon their natural rights; they argued that they had been taken from their
native lands, "where (though ignorance and unchristianity prevailed) they
were born free," to a land "where (though knowledge, Christianity, and
Freedom are their boast) they are compelled . . . to drag on their lives in miserable servitude."[2] The hypocrisy that did not escape the slaves somehow was
not persuasive to their masters, for the state legislature tabled the matter.
Nonetheless, the revenue laws that treated slaves as property were removed
by 1789, and bondage in the state was left alone to wither and die, which it did
sometime in the early nineteenth century.

In Rhode Island and Connecticut another type of compromise—gradual
emancipation—marked the end of slavery. After the Rhode Island legislature
failed to agree on outright abolition in 1784, it passed a gradual plan for emancipation. All Negro children born after 1 March 1784 would be freed, but each
would be required to serve the family of their mother's owner until they
reached maturity. The Connecticut legislature, responding to several slave
petitions for freedom, in 1777 made it easier to manumit slaves; in 1779 and
1780 the legislature considered but rejected plans for gradual abolition, then
finally adopted such a measure in 1784. Slaveholding swiftly declined in the
two New England states, but as late as 1810 there were still 108 slaves in
Rhode Island and 310 in Connecticut.

There were nearly 14,000 free blacks in 1790 in New York, New Jersey,
and Pennsylvania, along with some 36,000 blacks working their way out of
slavery through a system of gradual emancipation that did not free them until
a number of years of service were over (see table 20.1). Slaves who were children when emancipation bills passed in these states usually had to work without wages until they were in their middle or late twenties.

The middle states' system of gradual emancipation, like those of
Connecticut and Rhode Island, reflected the ideological essence and practical realities of the American Revolution. Although the Revolution was ideo-
logically based on principles of political rights and freedoms, it was even
more strongly grounded on a commitment to individual property rights.
Slaves would be freed, but only after most masters had worked them long
enough to be certain that no money was lost on their original investments.
Children, being more easily exploited, would continue to work as slaves
until they were adults. Up close, northern emancipation looks far less noble
than it does from afar.

Yet, by compromising between theoretical rights and practical economic realities, northern blacks and white fellow abolitionists were able to bring off a major achievement. Slavery ended in the North because, in effect, the slaves were willing to free themselves by purchasing liberty with their own labor. Instead of adamantly arguing for emancipation on unyielding moral grounds, as many abolitionists did prior to the Civil War, black and white abolitionists of the revolutionary era were more pragmatic. Dogmatically defining slavery as sin would have made the issue difficult to resolve, but approaching it as a political-economic issue permitted the compromise of gradual emancipation in the states where compromise was possible.

Farther to the south compromise was not possible. Although some slave owners may have realized the inconsistency of their positions on liberty and bondage, the economics of their position made most unwilling to make any concessions during their own lifetimes. Virginia, however, did go so far as to make manumissions feasible. A 1723 law had made it illegal for any Virginia master to emancipate a slave, but in 1782, swayed by a growing revolutionary uncertainty about holding bondspeople, legislators gave slaveholders the right to free slaves by will or by formal notice. Thousands were freed in the following years, so that by 1790 there were some 30,000 free blacks in the upper South. the area from North Carolina to Delaware. At the same time, however, there were still over 500,000 slaves in the region. In subsequent years the new state legislature of Virginia would receive proslavery appeals designed to stop further inroads into bondage rather than the freedom petitions more typical farther north.

South Carolina and Georgia had slightly over 2,000 free Negroes in 1790, but they were only a tiny minority, mostly located around Charleston, in a vast sea of over 136,000 African American slaves (see table 20.1). Southern whites claimed that their property rights in bondspeople were essential to their individual rights as citizens. Northern political leaders of the new republic were not willing to challenge this idea if the cost was going to be the political dissolution of the nation, especially since they had not yet resolved the issue in their own home states.

The limited willingness of white politicians to deal with the issue is symbolized in the compromises of the Constitutional Convention of 1787. The word *slave* does not even appear in this distinguished document; a variety of disingenuous euphemisms are used instead, such as "person held to service" and "other persons." For instance, the Constitution prohibited Congress from ending the importation of new slaves for 20 years in these words: "The migration or importation of such persons as any of the States now existing shall think proper to admit shall not be prohibited by the Congress prior to the year 1808." Slaves were counted as "three-fifths of all other persons" in determining the amount of representation each state received and what their proportionate share of direct taxes would be. This formulation did not mean that the Founding Fathers thought blacks were 60 percent human; the figure was based on a compromise over how to tax slave states where bondspeople were part of the wealth but not direct taxpayers themselves. In the new Constitution, masters were also given the right to reclaim any "person held to service"—that is, fugitive slaves.

Americans like to remember that John Hancock signed the Declaration of Independence in bold letters so that the king could not miss his intention, but the Founding Fathers were much less open about their support of continuing bondage. Their weaseling obfuscations should not be permitted to cloud our understanding that when the new government of the United States was formed, it was firmly committed to the defense of a racist caste system that betrayed the natural rights ideology of the American Revolution.

Part Six

Looking Forward

twenty-one

New Directions in a New Nation

Whereas Absalom Jones and Richard Allen, . . . from a love to the people of their complexion whom they beheld with sorrow, because of their irreligious and uncivilized state, often communed together upon this painful and important subject in order to form some kind of religious society, but there being too few to be found under the like concern, and those who were, differed in their religious sentiments; with these circumstances they labored for some time, till it was proposed . . . that a society should be formed, without regard to religious tenets, provided, the persons lived an orderly and sober life, in order to support one another for the benefit of their widows and fatherless children.

Preamble to the Rules of the Philadelphia Free African Society
(1787)

The petition of a great number of blacks, freemen of this Commonwealth, humbly shewth, that your petitioners are held in common with other freemen of this town and Commonwealth and have never been backward in paying our proportionate part of the burdens under which they have, or may labor under; and as we are willing to pay our equal part of these burdens, we are of the humble opinion that we have the right to enjoy the privileges of free men. But that we do not will appear in many instances, and we beg leave to mention one out of many, and that is the education of our children which now receive no benefit from the free schools in the town of Boston, which we think is a great grievance, as by woeful experience we now feel the want of a common education. We must, therefore, fear for our rising offspring to see them in ignorance in a land of gospel light when there is provision made for them as well as others and yet can't enjoy them, and for no other reason can be given this [than] they are black.

> Petition of a great number of blacks, freemen of this Commonwealth, to the state legislature of Massachusetts
> (1787)

Lieutenant Governor Gill of New Hampshire had both hired men and a slave to tend his farm. Gill, the story goes, rose early with his laborers and praying before breakfast and work, he thanked God that he had preserved them through the night and had given them to see another morning. At the close of the prayer his slave chided, "No morning yet, Massa."

> Paul Coffin, "Journal" (1795)

When a revolutionary American nationality began developing in the late eighteenth century, African Americans were already ahead of the curve. African immigrants had not passed on their tribal ethnicities or their languages to their American-born children, and the names they gave their sons and daughters, like the freedom names they took for themselves, were for the most part Anglo-American and assimilationist. But during the American Revolution the clear disparity between the theory of natural rights that underlay colonial calls for political independence and the diminished reality of racial caste and racist bondage experienced by African Americans put a double face on black political strategy. On the one hand, blacks took up arms and fought willingly and eagerly for their own freedom as members of both the patriot and British forces; they also petitioned for personal liberty and citizenship on the basis of the democratic ideals of the Revolution. On the other hand, they began to lose faith in the possibility that they would ever be accepted as equals into a multiracial American society; they were especially frustrated that their children were not being given an equal chance to succeed as citizens.

Blacks responded to these divergent forces with overt expressions of African American nationalism, building on a tradition of self-help by developing ethnically based institutions such as the First African Church of Savannah, the Brown Fellowship Society of Charleston, the African Society of Providence, the Free African Society of Philadelphia, and African Lodge No. 1 in Boston. It is important to understand that the word *African* in these names did not refer to the homelands. To the contrary, these organizations were developed by the most assimilated Negroes—"We the free Africans and their descendants," as the preamble for the Free African Society of Philadelphia put it. What, then, did *African* mean to these basically assimilationist organizations? It symbolized a proud assertion of the very cultural and racial identity that increasingly segregationist whites had been attacking as inferior and indelible.

The Revolution had called forth a new nationality in the colonies, but for African Americans, that nationality had two aspects. Thus, the new black organizations were both assimilationist and separatist. They accepted far more of Euro-American culture than they rejected, but what they clearly renounced was the racism that tarnished the otherwise universal values of revolutionary America. The colonial black urban elite accepted the American vision of progress and Christian morality, but on their own terms as independent African Americans, not as slaves or second-class citizens. Thus, they came to see themselves as a nationality within a nationality; blacks in the colonies had become African Americans in name as well as in fact.

It is interesting that in North America, blacks developed a sense of American nationality far quicker than their white countrymen or their black kinsmen in the Caribbean. Specific African ethnic identities had rapidly lost importance in the mainland English colonies; they no longer seemed particularly relevant to either blacks or whites. The physical realities of isolation and separation from their former countrymen required that social activities have a continental rather than a national flavor, and so the first generation of African Americans quickly found their commonalties more important than their differences. Many, if not most, Negro marriages in the colonies were mixed in terms of the spouses' original African nationalities. Under slavery whites treated all blacks as belonging to a single group determined solely by race; this racialist attitude combined with black compromises to form a new African American consciousness flowing out of a pan-African racial awareness.

This new American national consciousness among blacks blossomed a good century before a similar consciousness took hold among Anglo-Americans. Although blacks quickly came to accept themselves as Americans, some of the civic experiences our nation has deemed essential to the process of becoming American—frontier egalitarianism, remarkable economic opportunities, unprecedented political autonomy, and exceptional social mobility—were nevertheless all denied even to the most prosperous of the freeborn African American elite.

Black aspirations were torn between acceptance of the ideals American society preached and rejection of the cruelties American society practiced. It is little wonder that African American frustrations were coming to a nationalist boil as the colonial era ended. From out of this turmoil would arise during the early republic a three-pronged critical reaction to American culture: the special theology and practice of the black church, the satiric style in African American music, and a jeremiadic tradition among African American intellectuals of being intensely critical of the meaning of America.

At the vanguard of the emerging critical Afro-American consciousness was the small, free black urban community. These men and women were trying to make their living smack at the spot where malicious reality met fondest hope, right where the American nut would crack. For them, the ideals of the American Revolution had not been fulfilled with independence from Great

Britain. Two centuries later President Ronald Reagan would adopt the campaign slogan "It's morning again in America." But African Americans had, and have, a different idea about the dawn of freedom; as Lieutenant Governor Gill's slave told him soon after the birth of this nation, "No morning yet, Massa."

Free Negroes

> Those Negroes who keep shops live moderately, and never augment their business beyond a certain point. The reason is obvious; the whites . . . like not to give them credit to enable them to undertake any extensive commerce nor even to give them means of a common education by receiving them into their counting houses.
>
> J. P. Brissot de Warville, *New Travels in the United States of America* (1788)

By 1790 the colonial period had ended, yet the majority of African Americans remained enslaved, despite the noble principles of the Declaration of Independence and the Revolutionary War for American freedom. Only some 60,000 blacks in a population of around 760,000 African Americans were nominally free; that is, only about 8 percent of the black population was legally independent, a figure only a few percentage points higher than it had been just before the great war. Moreover, because of the caste nature of American society, even these free African Americans remained caught in a social and political limbo somewhere between slave status and the lowest stratum of free white society.

Traditionally free blacks had been included in restrictive codes designed to control the behavior of slaves and Indians because they were seen as potentially dangerous to the slave system. And as the colonial era ended, many black children who had been given their nominal freedom continued to be bound out to work for white families under indentures until they were 21. Socially American society had not yet adjusted to the implications of black freedom. In the extremely suggestive social pecking order of church seating, free Negroes were still usually placed with the bondspeople at the back of the church or in the balcony.

The Great Awakening had led to the formation of several early African American Baptist churches out of plantation congregations in Lunenburg and Williamsburg, Virginia, and Silver Bluff, South Carolina, but most black Christians retained institutional affiliations with white-dominated churches until the first years of the early republic. The early Methodist meetinghouses were more welcoming than most churches to black congregants but even there church classes were often segregated by race. Such un-

Christian practices as segregated seating were especially galling to the black elite, who were trying so hard to be accepted by their white counterparts.

Eventually, it all became too much to accept, and in 1785 Baltimore's black Methodists pulled away to form the Colored Methodist Society, an organization that would later give rise to the first black Methodist churches in the South. Similar difficulties in Philadelphia led the African American preacher Richard Allen to suggest the formation of a Negro church in 1787, although at first, because of denominational differences in the black community, only a nonsectarian African American society was formed.

Gaining freedom did not make colonial blacks any more equal before the law than they were in the eyes of God's prejudiced white deacons: African Americans were commonly denied the right to serve on juries, the right to receive public education, and even the right to vote (only five of the original thirteen states permitted black voting). Some communities even went so far as to try to ban blacks from buying property. Free Negroes were often discriminated against in gaining apprenticeships and jobs that were considered more skilled. Moneylenders refused to make business loans to black entrepreneurs, so that in America, where economic advancement determined social advancement, African Americans were forced to play in a rigged game that would doom many of them to smaller and smaller economic importance in the early republic. Nonetheless, as citizens, blacks were required to pay their full share of taxes.

In the colonial North a number of free blacks made a satisfactory living as personal servants, restaurateurs and caterers, barbers, and small shopkeepers, but far more struggled along barely able to make ends meet as common laborers, waiters, cooks, servants, woodcutters, boot blacks, chimney sweeps, seamen, seamstresses, and washerwomen. In the South most nonenslaved Negroes were small farmers or semiskilled workers; only rarely did they own any property besides a little land and a few personal possessions.

The richest of the colonial era's free blacks were urban dwellers who, although poor in relation to the white middle class, were literate members of a small but growing African American elite. Exceptional were free black planters like the African American gentleman in Prince Frederick Parish, South Carolina, who in 1786 owned 130 acres and five slaves, or another in Saint Paul Parish in Charleston District, South Carolina, who was reported in 1790 to have multiple plantations and 200 slaves.

As these examples suggest, slavery remained normal enough in the colonial era that the richest free blacks sometimes acquired slaves to help them in their labors so they could compete economically with white slaveholding planters. Throughout the colonies free Negroes also sometimes purchased as "slaves" spouses or other loved ones to avoid certain obligatory legal costs that discouraged the freeing of bondspeople. Thus, as late as 1790 six Negro families in Connecticut were still listed as slave owners. In the colonial era slavery was a legal institution both in Africa and in the English colonies of North America, and although African Americans were among the first to attack the system as a violation of natural rights, others in the black community were able to tolerate humane forms of bondage similar to those in Africa.

Nevertheless, black acceptance of slavery very rapidly evaporated in the early republic, especially among the free population of the northern states. There black leaders were starting a struggle against bondage that would not end until all African Americans were free. For some, however, the biggest question was whether such freedom could ever be truly achieved in the United States.

A Return to Africa?

> We are willing to submit to such regulations and laws, as may be made relative to us, until we leave the province, which we determine to do as soon as we can from our joynt labours procure money to transport ourselves to some part of the Coast of *Africa*, where we propose a settlement.
>
> Peter Bestes, Sambo Freeman, Felix Holbrook, and Chester Joie of Boston, freedom petition (20 April 1773)

The intellectual and social ferment of the revolutionary era inspired a powerful spirit of African American nationalism within the more radical members of the free black population of the North. The freedom petition of 1773 by four Massachusetts blacks, quoted above, illustrates a consciousness that was certainly more African American than African, for original African national identities had been displaced by a continental identification. The petition also reveals a powerful alienation from white-dominated society. This early pan-African consciousness was certainly something new.

The petitioners argued for their right to freedom based upon the revolutionary principles then pervading the colonies, but they did not identify with the goal of a new American nation; instead, they proposed that once they had gained their liberty they would leave America and "settle" in Africa as Westernized Christian colonizers. The particular locale in Africa of their settlement was not important to them.

The revolutionary concept of settling in Africa was not at all the same thing as the more reactionary idea of returning to Africa. These early African American nationalists, like most others of the period, did not intend to seek out their old ancestral homelands or ways of life; instead, they intended to enter Africa as progressive American colonists, Christians, and cultural missionaries, much like the later settlers of Liberia.

The Africa they had left, a land they now saw as blighted by paganism, despotism, slave trading, and inferior technology, no longer had much appeal to them. They wished to create a new Africa where they could achieve their

American-born dreams undeterred by the prejudices of a racist caste system. These early nationalists wished to live among fellow Africans essentially as African Americans, carrying the best parts of the American way of life to a land where the impediments of racial caste would no longer exist. This aspect of their late eighteenth-century African American nationalism seems a precursor to the nineteenth-century colonization ideas of Paul Cuffe, Martin Delany, and Robert Campbell, but it clearly was not a prototype of romantic twentieth-century Afrocentric nationalism, which emphasizes reviving an African cultural ideal unsullied by Western ways.

Even at the radical edge of their new nationalism, late eighteenth-century African Americans were as American as they were African. In fact, this identification was to be their special strength, for it would allow them in the years that followed to develop a variant of American culture that was less acquisitive and thereby truer to the most humane ideals of the new nation.

Conclusion

My position is a split one. I'm black. I'm a man of the West. These hard facts are bound to condition . . . my outlook. I see and understand the West; but I also see and understand the non- or anti-Western point of view. How is this possible? This double vision of mine stems from my being a product of Western civilization and from my racial identity. . . . Being a Negro living in a white Western Christian society, I've never been allowed to blend, in a natural and healthy manner, with the culture and civilization of the West. This contradiction of being both Western and a man of color creates a psychological distance, so to speak, between me and my environment. I'm self-conscious. I admit it. Yet I feel no need to apologize for it. Hence though Western, I'm inevitably critical of the West. Indeed, a vital element of my Westernness resides in this chronically skeptical, this irredeemably critical, outlook. I'm restless. I question not only myself, but my environment.

Richard Wright, "Tradition and Industrialization" (1957)

Looking back at the colonial period, we have come to see that men and women of African ancestry began arriving in the lands that would become the United States long before the English, Scots, Irish, and Germans, who are often portrayed as founders of the American nation. Not only were African Americans earlier to arrive than most immigrants, they were also more important. From the arrival of the *Mayflower* to the successful conclusion of the American Revolution, the colonial elite considered black slave labor in North America and the Caribbean absolutely essential to colonial economic success, and there is no doubt that the rapid expansion of the North American colonial economy was indeed critically dependent upon the labor of African colonists.

By 1750 roughly one in every five colonials in English North America, excluding Native Americans, was African American. Given both the numbers and the economic and cultural importance of America's early black population, to overlook the African American experience is to misunderstand a central factor of colonial history and the foundation of American democracy. America would not have been America without its interracial character.

All of the original 13 colonies profited from African slave labor, as did nearby Florida, Louisiana, and the southwestern borderlands. In some areas, such as South Carolina, blacks were the majority population throughout much of the colonial era, and their African cultural inheritance shaped the developing culture of the southern region far more than we previously thought. Moreover, the technical knowledge of African Americans was as integral to the economic maturation of the American colonies as their labor. Without this African intellectual contribution, the North American colonies would not have had the economic strength to break free from England during the American Revolution.

The first English arrivals on our shores had not planned to build a system of perpetual racial bondage, for they lacked national precedents for either slavery or caste. But tempting models of economic exploitation in the nearby West Indies and the dangers of class insurrection at home quickly led white authorities in North America to try to solve their problems of labor, capital accumulation, and political instability by adopting race-based slavery. It worked in the short run, but at a cost so huge as to all but morally bankrupt the country; indeed, we are still making regular payments on the mountain of social debt created when our nation's white Founding Fathers decided—looking back to precedents as old as Greece and Rome—that a dynamic, egalitarian, laissez-faire democracy could be based upon a system of immutable caste, chattel slavery, and economic exclusion.

Should we be surprised that it did not work? The white elite of early America created a monster: a physically vibrant and powerful nation that lacked a soul. They gave the new nation two brains: one, remaining nobly isolated from physical reality, proclaimed a revolutionary ideology of human freedom and dignity, while the other, a pea-sized and atavistic remnant of caste and coercion, directed the political economy with a cold-blooded, self-seeking, reptilian consciousness that belied the higher humanism of the revolutionary ideals.

Certainly the colonial period was an era of experimentation. Peoples with no long-standing history of interaction were being brought together in a difficult new environment. The result was a dynamic synergy. The unprecedented blending of traditions and insights from three continents created in America something new and remarkably successful, far more so than any one culture could have achieved alone.

There is no doubt that the English North American colonies gained dynamism and wealth by combining African practical knowledge with the

British desire for profits. But like the early atomic scientists who tickled the dragon's nose of nuclear energy while trying to avoid the ultimate explosion, the small elite class of slaveholders tried to exploit a labor system that was becoming ever more dangerously unstable. For a time they succeeded, but as with atomic energy's by-product of invisible and deadly radiation, there was an unexpected cost: a corroding racism that insidiously weakened the surrounding democratic structures, letting brittleness and decay set in and spreading an unforeseen moral cancer through the American system.

It is interesting in this regard to compare the English record with that of the surrounding borderlands, where blacks who settled among the Spanish and Native American populations had quite a different experience. African Americans in those areas quickly blended into the majority cultures. There are no black Chicano communities in Florida, Texas, or California, no African–Native-American subgroups among the tribes of the Southeast. Many factors surely help account for this African assimilation among the non-English populations of North America, but the nonracialist attitudes of African Americans and Native Americans were crucial.

Ironically, if English North America had not developed a white-supremacist racial caste system, African American culture might have had less influence on the wider American culture, and the world, because a separate African American consciousness would have ceased to exist and with it much of American culture's essential creativity. As it was, race came to matter.

The Africans who settled in English North America were not invited to the table. The Anglo-American groaning board at which white colonials feasted with such abandon had places for only the privileged race; blacks could stand behind and serve, but that was all. Should it be surprising that the thin cultural gruel slopped onto the plates of slaves seemed tasteless and unpalatable in comparison to the rich fare made exclusively available to whites? No wonder African Americans continued to savor their own sustaining traditions. They were willing to share their inheritance, but too many of the leftover dishes that came to them from the white man's table seemed tainted by a mean-spirited charity that begrudged blacks even secondhand opportunity.

A functional African American culture developed during the colonial era because blacks were not permitted to assimilate as equals; as a result, African cultural retentions survived more easily within an artificially separated black community, and African American culture treated English cultural ideas with more circumspection because of their connection to white slaveholders. Because African culture was effectively granted a protected caste environment in which to adjust to the new American multiculturalism, it did not wither away but grew stronger in its ensuing African American forms.

By the end of the colonial era North American whites were worried that the two cultures their slave system had created could not blend into one national culture. In 1782 Thomas Jefferson had come to the conclusion that the American experiment with racial slavery would probably end badly:

"Deep rooted prejudices entertained by the whites; ten thousand recollections, by the blacks, of the injuries they have sustained; new provocations; the real distinction which nature has made; and many other circumstances, will divide us into parties, and produce convulsions which will probably never end but in the extermination of the one or the other race."[1]

The colonial decisions about bondage that soured the American future were not inevitable and were chosen for the basest of motives. Slavery became essential to the development of colonial wealth, but as a consequence the young American republic would have its teeth set on edge. Confronting the evil of slavery was a matter of justice, for as the old New England slave put it, "Massa eat the meat, he now pick the bone."

Notes and References

Chapter 2

1. Quoted in E. W. Bovill, *The Golden Trade of the Moors*, 2d ed., rev. (New York, 1970), 90.

2. Francis Moore, *Travels into the Inland Parts of Africa* (London, 1738), 43.

Chapter 3

1. Quoted in Philip D. Curtin, ed., *Africa Remembered: Narratives by West Africans from the Era of the Slave Trade* (Madison, 1968), 78, based on excerpts from Equiano's *The Interesting Narrative of Olaudah Equiano, or Gustavus Vasa, the African*, 2 vols. (London, 1789).

2. Ibid., 72–73.

3. Ibid., 72.

Chapter 4

1. Quoted in Elizabeth Donnan, ed., *Documents Illustrative of the Slave Trade to America*, 4 vols. (Washington, D.C., 1935), 4:599.

2. Quoted in Curtin, *Africa Remembered*, 77.

Chapter 5

1. Quoted in Robert Edgar Conrad, ed., *Children of God's Fire* (Princeton, N.J., 1983), 26.

2. Quoted in Sidney and Emma Nogrady Kaplan, *The Black Presence in the Era of the American Revolution* (Amherst, Mass., 1989), 243.

3. Quoted in Curtin, *Africa Remembered*, 92.

4. Quoted in David Northrup, ed., *The Atlantic Slave Trade* (Lexington, Mass., 1994), 84.

5. Ibid., 87.

6. Ibid., 85.

Chapter 6

1. Quoted in Morris Bishop, *The Odyssey of Cabeza de Vaca* (New York, 1933), 138.

2. For the population of the colonial non-English frontier, see Peter H. Wood, "The Changing Population of the Colonial South: An Overview by Race and Region, 1685–1790," in Peter H. Wood, Gregory A. Waselkov, and M. Thomas Hatley, eds., *Powhatan's Mantle: Indians in the Colonial Southeast* (Lincoln, 1989), 38–39.

3. J. Leitch Wright, Jr., "British East Florida: Loyalist Bastion," in Samuel Proctor, ed., *Eighteenth Century Florida: The Impact of the American Revolution* (Gainesville, 1978): 8–9.

4. Hall, *Africans in Colonial Louisiana* (Baton Rouge, La., 1992), 279.

Chapter 7

1. Hall, *Africans in Colonial Louisiana*, 10.

2. Ibid., 103.

3. Robert L. Jenkins, "Africans in Colonial and Territorial Mississippi," in Barbara Carpenter, ed., *Ethnic Heritage in Mississippi* (Jackson, 1992).

4. Quoted in William Loren Katz, *The Black West* (Seattle, 1987), 12.

Chapter 9

1. Quoted in Lorenzo Johnston Greene, *The Negro in Colonial New England* (1942; reprint, New York, 1969), 60.

Chapter 10

1. Quoted in Edgar J. McManus, *Black Bondage in the North* (Syracuse, N.Y., 1973), 5.

Chapter 11

1. For these advertisements and others, see Gerald W. Mullin, *Flight and Rebellion: Slave Resistance in Eighteenth-Century Virginia* (New York, 1972), 97, 73.

2. Quoted in Allan Kulikoff, *Tobacco and Slaves: The Development of Southern Cultures in the Chesapeake, 1680–1800* (Chapel Hill, N.C., 1986), 66.

3. Ibid., 73.

4. Quoted in Jon Sensbach, *African-Americans in Salem* (Winston-Salem, N.C., n.d.), 12.

Chapter 12

1. Peter H. Wood, *Black Majority: Negroes in Colonial South Carolina from 1670 through the Stono Rebellion* (New York, 1974), 31.

2. Daniel C. Littlefield, *Rice and Slaves: Ethnicity and the Slave Trade in Colonial South Carolina* (Urbana, 1991), 96–98, 103–5.

3. Quoted in Michael Mullin, *Africa in America: Slave Acculturation and Resistance in the American South and the British Caribbean, 1736–1831* (Urbana, Ill., 1992), 187.

4. Quoted in Robert L. Jenkins, "Africans in Colonial and Territorial Mississippi," in Barbara Carpenter, ed., *Ethnic Heritage in Mississippi* (Jackson, Miss., 1992), 133.

Chapter 13

1. William J. Brown, *The Life of William J. Brown of Providence, R. I.* (Providence, 1883), 10–11.

2. John Brickell, *The Natural History of North Carolina* (1737; reprint, Raleigh, N.C., 1911), 357.

3. Quoted in Daniel H. Usner, Jr., *Indians, Settlers, and Slaves in a Frontier Exchange Economy* (Chapel Hill, N.C., 1992), 59.

4. Ibid., 73.

Chapter 14

1. Quoted in Winthrop D. Jordan, *White over Black? American Attitudes toward the Negro, 1550–1812* (Baltimore, 1968), 184.

2. Quoted in John W. Blassingame, *Slave Testimony* (Baton Rouge, La., 1977), 33.

3. Quoted in Mechal Sobel, *The World They Made Together* (Princeton, N.J., 1987), 137.

4. Quoted in William D. Piersen, *Black Legacy: America's Hidden Heritage* (Amherst, Mass., 1993), 158.

5. Quoted in ibid., 160.

6. Quoted in Lawrence A. Cremin, *American Education: The Colonial Experience* (New York, 1970), 533.

7. Quoted in Ulrich B. Phillips, *Life and Labor in the Old South* (1929; reprint, Boston, 1963), 195.

8. Quoted in William D. Piersen, *Black Yankees: The Development of an Afro-American Subculture in Eighteenth-Century New England* (Amherst, Mass., 1988), 40–41.

9. Olaudah Equiano, *Equiano's Travels*, ed. Paul Edwards (1789; reprint, London, 1967), 43.

10. Quoted in Piersen, *Black Yankees*, 39.

11. Quoted in ibid., 91.

12. Quoted in Frank J. Klingberg, *An Appraisal of the Negro in Colonial South Carolina* (Washington, D.C., 1941), 14.

13. Mullin, *Africa in America*, 170, 167.

Chapter 15

1. Quoted in Gary B. Nash, *Forging Freedom: The Formation of Philadelphia's Black Community 1720–1840* (Cambridge, Mass., 1988), 13.

2. Peter Kalm, *Peter Kalm's Travels in North America*, 2 vols. (New York, 1937), 1:210.

3. Quoted in Jordan, *White over Black*, 202–3.

4. Klingberg, *An Appraisal of the Negro in Colonial South Carolina*, 87.

5. Quoted in Piersen, *Black Yankees*, 49.

6. Quoted in Dena J. Epstein, *Sinful Tunes and Spirituals: Black Fold Music to the Civil War* (Urbana, Ill., 1977), 104.

Chaper 16

1. Quoted in Piersen, *Black Legacy*, 68.

2. Shane White, *Somewhat More Independent: The End of Slavery in New York City, 1770–1810* (Athens, Ga., 1991), 97.

3. Quoted in J. L. Dillard, *Black English* (New York, 1972), 89.

4. Quoted in Piersen, *Black Yankees*, 109.

5. Ibid.

6. Ibid., 106.

Chapter 17

1. Quoted in Piersen, *Black Yankees*, 100.
2. Quoted in Ulrich B. Phillips, *American Negro Slavery* (1918; reprint, Baton Rouge, La., 1966), 20.
3. *South Carolina Gazette*, 15 October 1772, as quoted in Leila Sellers, *Charleston Business on the Eve of the American Revolution* (Chapel Hill, N.C., 1934), 107.
4. Quoted in Epstein, *Sinful Tunes and Spirituals*, 38.
5. *South Carolina Gazette*, 17 September 1772, as quoted in Peter H. Wood, *Black Majority*, 342.

Chapter 18

1. *The Life and Selected Writings of Thomas Jefferson*, ed. Adrienne Koch and William Peden (New York, 1944), 278.
2. Quoted in Mullin, *Flight and Rebellion*, 74.

Chapter 19

1. Quoted in Herbert Aptheker, *American Negro Slave Revolts* (New York, 1943), 80.
2. John Brickell, *The Natural History of North Carolina* (1737; Murfreesboro, N.C., 1968), 357.
3. Henry Laurens, letter to John Lewis Gervais, 29 January 1766, *The Papers of Henry Laurens*, 14 vols., George C. Rogers, ed., (Columbia, 1974), 5:53.
4. Quoted in Peter H. Wood, "'The Dream Deferred': Black Freedom Struggles on the Eve of White Independence," in Gary Y. Okihiro, ed., *In Resistance: Studies in African, Caribbean, and Afro-American History* (Amherst, Mass., 1986), 171.
5. Ibid., 175.
6. Benjamin Quarles, *The Negro in the American Revolution* (New York, 1973), vii.

Chapter 20

1. Quoted in Arthur Zilversmit, *The First Emancipation: The Abolition of Slavery in the North* (Chicago, 1967), 112.
2. Quoted in ibid., 116–17.

Conclusion

1. Thomas Jefferson, *Notes on Virginia*, quoted in Jordan, *White over Black*, 436.

Bibliographical Essay

General Works

A good starting guide for suggestions for further reading in the African American history of the colonial era is Donald R. Wright, *African Americans in the Colonial Era: From African Origins through the American Revolution* (Arlington Heights, Ill., 1990), which judiciously surveys the important historical issues and places the relevant scholarly works into a useful context; a special strength is Wright's own expertise in African history and culture. Peter Kolchin, *American Slavery 1619–1877* (New York, 1993), also has a good general survey of the era in its first three chapters and includes a well-selected bibliographical essay.

For a more detailed bibliographical introduction to the historiography of early African American history, see Peter H. Wood, "'I Did the Best I Could for My Day': The Study of Early Black History during the Second Reconstruction, 1960 to 1976," *William and Mary Quarterly*, third series 35, no. 2 (April 1978): 185–225. Wood's article can be updated with later works such as the more recent list of articles on slavery in Paul Finkleman, *Articles on American Slavery 3: Colonial Southern Slavery* (New York, 1989). An early classic study, now dated in its perspective but still useful in its coverage, is Ulrich B. Phillips, *American Negro Slavery* (1918; reprint Baton Rouge, 1969).

The most influential scheme of cultural periodization for colonial African American history was developed by Ira Berlin, "Time, Space, and the Evolution of Afro-American Society in British Mainland North America," *American Historical Review* 85, no. 1 (February 1980): 44–78. An early and interesting attempt to put the African American experience in a context with Euro-American and Native American history is Gary B. Nash, *Red, White, and Black: The Early Peoples of America* (Englewood Cliffs, N.J., 1974).

The historical record should be complemented with the growing body of evidence being developed by American archaeologists. A good introduction to this work is Leland Ferguson, *Uncommon Ground: Archaeology and Early African America, 1650–1800* (Washington, D.C., 1992), which examines evidence from early African American lives—potsherds, postholes, pipes, beads, and food fragments—to illustrate African influences on eating habits, religion, and house construction. Ferguson covers the Atlantic coast from Virginia to Florida and pays special attention to Indian, European, and African interaction. Another interesting archaeological study is Robert L. Schuyler, ed., *Archaeological Perspectives on Ethnicity in America: Afro-American and Asian American Culture History* (Farmingdale, N.Y., 1980). Although only the first half of this book is devoted to African American culture, the essays on the African influence on Colono-Indian pottery and on Black Lucy's Garden in Andover, Massachusetts, are worth examining. See also Anne Elizabeth Yentsch, *A Chesapeake Family and Their Slaves* (Cambridge, Mass., 1994).

The African Homelands

Robert W. July, *Precolonial Africa: An Economic and Social History* (New York, 1975), offers an excellent and readable social-historical description of traditional Africa and its peoples during the era when North America was being colonized. For an introduction to traditional African religion, see John S. Mbiti, *African Religions and Philosophies* (New York, 1970). Original sources are also available, and the best general collection is Philip Curtin, ed., *Africa Remembered: Narratives by West Africans from the Era of the Slave Trade* (Madison, 1968), which includes among its well-annotated narratives three firsthand accounts of African life from victims of the eighteenth-century slave trade.

For the possibility of pre-Columbian African contacts with the Americas, see Ivan Van Sertima, *They Came before Columbus: The African Presence in Ancient America* (New York, 1977), and some of the suggestive work in Ivan Van Sertima, ed., *African Presence in Early America* (New Brunswick, N.J., 1992).

The Slave Trade

On the slave trade in general, a good introduction is Joseph C. Miller, "The Slave Trade," in *Encyclopedia of the North American Colonies*, 4 vols., ed. Jacob Ernest Cooke et al. (New York, 1993), 2:45–66. The fullest modern treatment of the slave trade to the North American colonies is James A. Rawley, *The Transatlantic Slave Trade: A History* (New York, 1981). Daniel P. Mannix, with Malcolm Cowley, *Black Cargoes: A History of the Atlantic Slave Trade, 1518–1865* (New York, 1962), also offers powerful descriptions of what the slave trade was really like. Olaudah Equiano, *The Interesting Narrative of the Life of Olaudah Equiano Written by Himself,* ed. Robert J. Allison (Boston, 1995), describes the African and Atlantic slave trades as experienced by one of the victims.

For students, David Northrup, ed., *The Atlantic Slave Trade* (Lexington, Mass., 1994), introduces the key issues and includes both primary and secondary readings. Also useful are Ira Berlin, "The Slave Trade and the Development of Afro-American Society in English Mainland North America, 1619–1775," *Southern Studies* 2, no. 3/4 (Fall/Winter 1991): 335–49; Steven Deyle, "'By Far the Most Profitable Trade': Slave Trading in British Colonial North America," *Slavery and Abolition* 10, no. 2 (August 1989): 107–25, a brief but updated survey of the colonial slave trade; and John Thornton, *Africa and Africans in the Making of the Atlantic World, 1400–1680* (Cambridge, Mass., 1992). For an interesting view of how Africans explained the slave trade, see William D. Piersen, *Black Legacy: America's Hidden Heritage* (Amherst, Mass., 1993).

The best introduction to the numbers of people shipped to America is Philip D. Curtin, *The African Slave Trade: A Census* (Madison, 1969), although refinements of the numbers are constantly being offered. For a general bibliography, see Joseph C. Miller, *Slavery: A Worldwide Bibliography, 1900–1982* (White Plains, N.Y., 1985). Annual supplements to this bibliography are available in the journal *Slavery and Abolition*.

There are also a number of good regional studies of the slave trade. See especially Jay Coughtry, *The Notorious Triangle: Rhode Island and the African Slave Trade, 1700–1807* (Philadelphia, 1981); Daniel C. Littlefield, "The Slave Trade to Colonial South Carolina: A Profile," *South Carolina Historical Magazine* 91, no. 2 (April 1990): 68–98; and Walter E. Minchinton, Celia King, and Peter Waite, eds., *Virginia Slave Trade Statistics, 1698–1775* (Richmond, 1984).

The Development of North American Slavery

For a good introductory discussion of the development of North American slavery, see Oscar Handlin and Mary F. Handlin, "Origins of the Southern Labor System," *William and Mary Quarterly* 7, no. 2 (April 1950), 199–222, who argue that slavery influenced the development of racism; their discussion can be usefully compared with Carl N. Degler, "Slavery and the Genesis of American Race Prejudice," *Comparative Studies in Society and History* 2, no. 1 (October 1959): 49–66, who reverses the argument. Winthrop D. Jordan, *White over Black: American Attitudes toward the Negro, 1550–1812* (Baltimore, 1968), presents a brilliant analysis of the complex interrelationship between racism and the development of American slavery; moreover, this book can be mined again and again for its wealth of related material on any number of subjects.

For the legal situation, see A. Leon Higginbotham, Jr., *In the Matter of Color: Race and the American Legal Process, the Colonial Period* (New York, 1978).

The Spanish Lands

Scholars of the Spanish borderlands have not been generally interested in the African Americans who were part of the experience. There are a few important exceptions. Richard R. Wright, "Negro Companions of the Spanish Explorers," *Phylon* 2, no. 4 (1941): 334–36, is an older and very brief study but still worth looking at. Jack D. Forbes, "Black Pioneers: The Spanish-Speaking Afroamericans of the Southwest," *Phylon* 27, no. 3 (Fall 1966): 233–46, is another pioneering and suggestive work.

The best contemporary examples are found in the scholarship of Jane Landers. See especially her "Gracia Real de Santa Teresa de Mose: A Free Black Town in Spanish Colonial America," *American Historical Review* 95, no. 1 (February 1990): 9–30; "Africans in the Land of Ayllón: The Exploration and Settlement of the Southeast," in *Columbus and the Land of Ayllón*, ed. Jeannine Cook (Mobile, Ala., 1992); and "Spanish Sanctuary: Fugitives in Florida, 1687–1790," *Florida Historical Quarterly* 62, no. 3 (January 1984): 296–313. See also Fray Angelico Chavez, "Pohé-Yemo's Representative and the Pueblo Revolt of 1680," *New Mexico Historical Review* 42, no. 2 (April 1967): 85–126, who did some fascinating detective work on the history of an Afro-Indian family of the seventeenth century. A broader perspective on Mexico is offered in Colin A. Palmer, *Slaves of the White God: Blacks in Mexico, 1570–1650* (Cambridge, Mass., 1976).

The French Lands

The best place to begin a study of the African American experience in the colonial French territories is Gwendolyn Midlo Hall, *Africans in Colonial Louisiana: The Development of Afro-Creole Culture in the Eighteenth Century* (Baton Rouge, 1992), an award-winning study of early Louisiana by a scholar familiar with the Caribbean and West Africa as well as the colonial sources of France and Spain. See also Daniel H. Usner, Jr., "From African Captivity to American Slavery: The Introduction of Black Laborers to Colonial Louisiana," *Louisiana History* 20, no. 1 (Winter 1979): 25–48, and Donald Everett, "Free People of Color in Colonial Louisiana," *Louisiana History* 7, no. 1 (Winter 1966): 5–20, which looks at the early years of one of the nation's most important free black communities.

New England

Any examination of black New England should begin with Lorenzo Johnston Greene, *The Negro in Colonial New England* (New York, 1942). This classic account of early New England is still well worth study, especially as regards the development of slavery in New England and the legal and social constraints of bondage. Greene should be supplemented with the more African-centered cultural insights of William D. Piersen, *Black Yankees: The Development of an Afro-American Subculture in Eighteenth-Century New England* (Amherst, Mass., 1988), which is especially useful for its analysis of the process by which African arrivals assimilated into, and changed, New England; of great interest is the discussion of the region's black kings and governors. See also Edgar J. McManus, *Black Bondage in the North* (Syracuse, N.Y., 1973), a strong, but brief, overview.

New York, New Jersey, and Pennsylvania

McManus's *Black Bondage in the North* is also a good starting point for an overview of colonial slavery in the northern middle colonies; it is clear, concise, and comprehensive. For deeper coverage of New York, see Edgar J. McManus, *A History of Negro Slavery in New York* (Syracuse, N.Y., 1966); Richard Shannon Moss, *Slavery on Long Island: A Study in Local Institutional and Early African-American Communal Life* (New York, 1993); Willie F. Page, "The African Slave during the Early English Period, 1664–1700," *Journal of the Afro-American Historical and Genealogical Society* 5 (1984): 123–32; A. J. Williams-Meyers, "Hands That Picked No Cotton: An Exploratory Examination of African Slave Labor in the Colonial Economy of the Hudson River Valley to 1800," *Afro-Americans in New York Life and History* 11, no. 11 (July 1987): 25–51; and Shane White, *Somewhat More Independent: The End of Slavery in New York City, 1770–1810* (Athens, Ga., 1991). White's discussion of the collapse of slavery in New York is weighted to the postcolonial period but has important insights on African American style—clothes, language, gesture—that cannot be found elsewhere.

For Pennsylvania, see Gary B. Nash, *Forging Freedom: The Formation of Philadelphia's Black Community, 1720–1840* (Cambridge, Mass., 1988), a wonderfully insightful book about African American urban life in early Philadelphia. Since Philadelphia experienced large-scale black immigration from the South, the city's problems have a resonance with modern urban concerns. See also Gary B. Nash, "Forging Freedom: The Emancipation Experience in the Northern Seaport Cities, 1775–1820," in *Slavery and Freedom in the Age of the American Revolution*, ed. Ira Berlin and Ronald Hoffman (Urbana, Ill., 1983), 3–48; Gary B. Nash and Jean R. Soderlund, *Freedom by Degrees: Emancipation in Pennsylvania and Its Aftermath* (New York, 1991); Alan Tully, "Patterns of Slaveholding in Colonial Pennsylvania: Chester and Lancaster Counties, 1729–1758," *Journal of Social History* 6, no. 3 (Spring 1973): 284–306; and Billy Smith and Richard Wojtowicz, "The Precarious Freedom of Blacks in the Mid-Atlantic Region: Excerpts from the *Pennsylvania Gazette*, 1728–1776," *Pennsylvania Magazine of History and Biography* 113, no. 2 (April 1989): 237–64, an article that puts a human face on the runaways who attempted to escape slavery.

Chesapeake

T. H. Breen and Stephen Innes, *"Myne Own Ground": Race and Freedom on Virginia's Eastern Shore, 1640–1676* (Oxford, 1980), is a fascinating look into the lives of upwardly mobile African Americans in the seventeenth century; this book demonstrates beyond doubt that American slavery and racial attitudes did not spring into life full-grown; instead, the peculiarly perverse American system of caste, coercion, and racial identity developed in response to declining economic opportunity for those at the bottom of society. In Allan Kulikoff,

Tobacco and Slaves: The Development of Southern Cultures in the Chesapeake, 1680–1800 (Chapel Hill, N.C., 1986), the large section on black Chesapeake society in the eighteenth century is essential reading.

For readers interested in early African American culture and its effects on white culture, two books by Mechal Sobel should not be missed: *The World They Made Together: Black and White Values in Eighteenth-Century Virginia* (Princeton, N.J., 1987), and *Trabelin' On: The Slave Journey to an Afro-Baptist Faith* (Princeton, N.J., 1988).

Other excellent work on the Chesapeake region is available. Richard S. Dunn, "Black Society in the Chesapeake, 1776–1810," in Berlin and Hoffman, *Slavery and Freedom*, 49–82; Rhys Isaac, *The Transformation of Virginia 1740–1790* (New York, 1988); Allan Kulikoff, "The Origins of Afro-American Society in Tidewater Maryland and Virginia, 1700–1790," *William and Mary Quarterly*, third series 35, no. 2 (April 1978): 226–59; Thad Tate, *The Negro in Eighteenth-Century Williamsburg* (Williamsburg, Va., 1965); Jon Sensbach, *African-Americans in Salem* (Winston-Salem, N.C., n.d); and Philip J. Schwartz, *Twice Condemned: Slaves and the Criminal Laws of Virginia, 1705–1865* (Baton Rouge, La., 1988), are all worth reading.

Two studies deserve special mention. Edmund S. Morgan, *American Slavery, American Freedom: The Ordeal of Colonial Virginia* (New York, 1975), suggests that Virginia's experiment in democracy could arise only after the laboring masses were no longer able to become a giddy revolutionary multitude; democratic freedom for middling whites depended upon the enslavement of caste-bound blacks. Gerald W. Mullin, *Flight and Rebellion: Slave Resistance in Eighteenth-Century Virginia* (New York, 1972), presents a packed and informative examination of the ways in which Virginia slaves resisted their bondage.

Lower South

The best vantage point for gaining insight into African American life in the lower South through a historical perspective is Peter H. Wood, *Black Majority: Negroes in Colonial South Carolina from 1670 through the Stono Rebellion* (New York, 1974). The economic importance of Africans to the economy is persuasively examined in Daniel C. Littlefield, *Rice and Slaves: Ethnicity and the Slave Trade in Colonial South Carolina* (Urbana, Ill., 1981). Robert L. Jenkins, "Africans in Colonial and Territorial Mississippi," in *Ethnic Heritage in Mississippi*, ed. Barbara Carpenter (Jackson, Miss., 1992), 126–54, offers clear and concise coverage of West Florida and the Natchez region.

Other important work on the lower South includes Joyce E. Chaplin, "Tidal Rice Cultivation and the Problem of Slavery in South Carolina and Georgia, 1760–1815," *William and Mary Quarterly*, third series 44, no. 1 (January 1992): 29–61; Russell R. Menard, "The Africanization of the Lowcountry Labor Force, 1670–1730," in *Race and Family in the Colonial South*, ed. Winthrop D. Jordan and Sheila L. Skemp (Jackson, Miss., 1987), 81–198;

Philip D. Morgan, "Black Society in the Lowcountry, 1760–1810," in Berlin and Hoffman, *Slavery and Freedom*, 83–141; Julia Floyd Smith, *Slavery and Rice Culture in Low Country Georgia, 1750–1860* (Knoxville, Tenn., 1985); and Betty Wood, *Slavery in Colonial Georgia, 1730–1775* (Athens, Ga., 1984).

African American Contact with Indians

We still have much to learn about African American and Native American contacts; some good places to begin are Jack D. Forbes, *Black Africans and Native Americans: Color, Race, and Caste in the Evolution of Red-Black Peoples* (New York, 1988); Jane Landers, "Black-Indian Interaction in Spanish Florida," *Colonial Latin American Historical Review* 2, no. 2 (Spring 1993); Kenneth W. Porter, "Relations between Negroes and Indians within the Present Limits of the United States," *Journal of Negro History* 17, no. 3 (July 1932): 287–369; William S. Willis, "Divide and Rule: Red, White, and Black in the Southeast," *Journal of Negro History* 48, no. 3 (July 1963): 157–76; and Daniel H. Usner, Jr., *Indians, Settlers, and Slaves in a Frontier Exchange Economy: The Lower Mississippi Valley before 1783* (Chapel Hill, N.C., 1992). Theda Purdue, *Slavery and the Evolution of Cherokee Society, 1540–1866* (Knoxville, Tenn., 1979), which examines early contacts between blacks and the Cherokee, is especially interesting for its comparison of African and Native American slavery.

African American Culture

The classic work on the African nature of early African American society and the importance of studying Africa as a source culture for America is Melville J. Herskovits, *The Myth of the Negro Past* (Boston, 1958). Many scholars suggest balancing Herskovits with the doubts of E. Franklin Frazier, *The Negro Family in the United States* (Chicago, 1939), but clearly Herskovits has won the argument over whether or not African cultures had influence on early African American life. A good theoretical introduction to key issues is the work of the anthropologists Sidney W. Mintz and Richard Price, *The Birth of African-American Culture: An Anthropological Perspective* (Boston, 1992).

There are also a number of studies that cover important aspects of this subject; see especially Mary Beth Norton, Herbert G. Gutman, and Ira Berlin, "The Afro-American Family in the Age of Revolution," 175–91, and Albert J. Roboteau, "The Slave Church in the Era of the American Revolution, 193–213, both in Berlin and Hoffman, *Slavery and Freedom*; Piersen, *Black Yankees*; Sobel, *The World They Made Together*; see also Sobel's *Trabelin' On*; John Vlach, *The Afro-American Tradition in the Decorative Arts* (Cleveland, 1978); White, *Somewhat More Independent*; Wood, *Black Majority*; and Michael J. Morgan, "Rock and Roll Unplugged: African-American Music in Eighteenth-Century America," *Eighteenth-Century Studies* 27, no. 4 (Summer 1994): 649–92. Although it spans beyond the colonial era, cultural connections to Africa are highlighted in Piersen, *Black Legacy*.

Resistance

Herbert Aptheker, *American Negro Slave Revolts* (New York, 1943), is still the indispensable starting point for those interested in African American resistance to slavery. An excellent modern introduction to the topic is Peter H. Wood, "Slave Resistance," in Cooke, *Encyclopedia of the North American Colonies*, 2:209–20. Many specialized works are also available. A good place to begin is with the Middle Passage; see Lorenzo J. Greene, "Mutiny on the Slave Ships," *Phylon* 5, no. 4 (Fourth Quarter 1944): 346–54; and Darold D. Wax, "Negro Resistance to the Early American Slave Trade," *Journal of Negro History* 51, no. 1 (January 1966): 1–15. The important New York revolts are covered in Kenneth Scott, "The Slave Insurrection in New York in 1712," *New York Historical Society Quarterly* 45, no. 1 (January 1961): 43–74; and Thomas J. Davis, *A Rumor of Revolt: The "Great Negro Plot" in Colonial New York* (New York, 1985). Several good studies of more southern rebellions are John K. Thornton, "African Dimensions of the Stono Rebellion," *American Historical Review* 96, no. 4 (October 1991): 1101–13, which takes seriously the African dimension of the early black experience; and Alan D. Watson, "Impulse toward Independence: Resistance and Rebellion among North Carolina Slaves 1750–1775," *Journal of Negro History* 63, no. 4 (Fall 1978): 317–28.

Running away was perhaps the most common form of overt resistance, and among the several good studies are Michael P. Johnson, "Runaway Slaves and the Slave Communities in South Carolina, 1799 to 1830," *William and Mary Quarterly*, Third series 38, no. 3 (July 1981): 418–41; and Mullin, *Flight and Rebellion*.

A broader comparative study with a great deal of useful detail is Michael Mullin, *Africa in America: Slave Acculturation and Resistance in the American South and the British Caribbean, 1736–1831* (Urbana, Ill., 1992), and similarly, Silvia R. Frey, *Water from the Rock: Black Resistance in a Revolutionary Age* (Princeton, N.J., 1991), treats a wide range of resistance forms around the time of the American Revolution.

The Revolutionary War Era

A good introduction to the African American issues of the revolutionary era is the chapter on the American Revolution in Kolchin, *American Slavery, 1619–1877*, which includes a good bibliography. For a comparative context, see David Brion Davis, *The Problem of Slavery in the Age of Revolution, 1770–1823* (Ithaca, N.Y., 1975). Two excellent monographs covering the period are Benjamin Quarles, *The Negro in the American Revolution* (New York, 1973), and Frey, *Water from the Rock*.

There are also a number of fine shorter essays available. See the collected essays in Berlin and Hoffman, *Slavery and Freedom;* Jacqueline Jones, "Race, Sex, and Self-Evident Truths: The Status of Slave Women during the Era of the American Revolution," in *Women in the Age of the American Revolution*, ed. Ronald Hoffman and Peter J. Albert (Charlottesville, Va., 1989).

These scholarly studies can be supplemented with the primary source material in Sidney Kaplan and Emma Nogrady Kaplan, *The Black Presence in the Era of the American Revolution* (Amherst, Mass., 1989), a book with a wonderful assortment of illustrations, documentary material, and short biographies of some African Americans from the revolutionary era. See also Gary B. Nash, *Race and Revolution* (Madison, 1990), a work especially noteworthy for its excellent collection of documents from the era relating to abolitionism, not to mention the three strong overview essays by the author.

The aftermath of the Revolution in the northern colonies is treated in Arthur Zilversmit, *The First Emancipation: The Abolition of Slavery in the North* (Chicago, 1967).

Index

The Author

_____

William D. Piersen has graduate degrees in folklore and African and American history from Indiana University. While at the Folklore Institute in Bloomington, he became interested in the connections between African and African American folklore and in the black kings and governors who ruled over early African American celebrations across the New World. His research led to a dissertation on black life in early New England and to articles in the *Journal of Negro History*, the *Journal of American Folklore*, and *Research in African Literatures*.

Professor Piersen is currently chairman of the history department at Fisk University, where he has taught for 17 years. His major historical publications include two books, *Black Yankees: The Development of an Afro-American Subculture in Eighteenth-Century New England* and *Black Legacy: America's Hidden Heritage*, which examine the formation of African American culture and the relationship of African American culture to the development of American culture as a whole.